Money, Thou Art Loosed!

by
Dr. Leroy Thompson Sr.

D0324487

Ever Increasing Word Ministries
Darrow, Louisiana

Unless otherwise indicated, all Scripture quotations in this volume are from the *King James Version* of the Bible.

First Printing 1999

ISBN 0-963-2584-4-3

Ever Increasing Word Ministries
P.O. Box 7
Darrow, Louisiana 70725

Contents

A few years ago, after I received the revelation of "Money cometh," the Lord begin to share with me key revelation and insight into the Word of God on another aspect of financial prosperity.

This revelation comes from a scripture that we normally look to for physical healing. The Lord spoke to me about the story of the woman who had a spirit of infirmity for eighteen years (Luke 13:12). He said to me, "Do you know that the Body of Christ has the same authority over money that they have over sickness and disease?" He then told me that we have authority over money and can make demands on money and that money would obey us.

Just as Jesus said, "Woman, thou art loosed from thine infirmity," the Lord is saying the same thing to us about the debt, poverty, and lack that has plagued the Body of Christ for years. He is saying, "Money, thou art loosed!"

I began meditating on what the Lord shared with me. In essence, the Spirit of God was saying that we have the ability to loose all the money that we need or desire in our lives by speaking His Word with the anointing.

In this book, we are going to deal with various principles of obtaining money God's way — of loosing money into our lives according to the Word of God. To receive financial prosperity, it is vitally important that we be in agreement with God's Word

on the subject. I am living in the God-kind of prosperity today —
in both my personal life and my ministry — because I learned to
agree with the Word of God concerning money.

If you've been struggling over a lack of money, God wants
to show you a better way. Your having money is important to
God. Your having money with the right intentions and attitudes
will put you in position to walk in the fullness of His abundance
for you and be a blessing to others. But, most importantly, your
prosperity will glorify God.

God desires that you be a master over money. He desires
that you know and exercise your authority over finances. When
you get clear this revelation about God's will for you financially,
money will have to follow you all the days of your life! So as
you read this book, set your heart to tap into the Word of God
and receive what is rightfully yours in Christ.

Money, thou art loosed!

One of the first things I have to deal with when I teach folks about prosperity is the fact that having money is just one aspect of prosperity, but it is one area that the Body of Christ as a whole has fallen short in. Some people get angry when I say that, but it's true; up to ninety percent of the Body of Christ is broke. Now when I say "broke," I don't mean that ninety percent of Christians live in poverty. If you have $5,000 or $10,000 in the bank, you're still broke. One doctor's bill could wipe that out for you!

Not being broke means having a *full* supply. That's what God wants for His children. And He has enough resources — enough deposits in the earth's realm — so that all of His children may be wealthy.

The Missing Ingredient

However, we are going to have to change our mindset about money in order to live in the fullness God wants us to have. The Body of Christ is full of "confession," but confession is not bringing the finances in like it should be. So there must be a missing link or ingredient that we can add to our confession that will cause money to come to us as God intended.

I believe that the missing ingredient in the lives of many believers is their having faith and being full of confidence that prosperity is the will of God for them.

For I know the thoughts that I think toward you, saith the Lord, thoughts of peace, and not of evil, to give you an expected end.

JEREMIAH 29:11

The first part of that verse says, **"For I know the thoughts that I think toward you, saith the Lord...."** You see, there's a certain way that God thinks about His children — a certain attitude that He has toward them. And this attitude describes the way God desires for His children to live.

There's certain provision that God has made for His children, but they will not enjoy it unless they know how to tap into it through thinking and acting in line with His Word. Many of us have come a long way from our traditional denominational backgrounds in which we grew up being taught that poverty was a mark of holiness. In other words, we were wrongly taught that the less you had, the closer you were to God.

But that is not God's plan for us. Jeremiah 29:11 says His plan is to prosper and do good unto us. God wants the best for us, because He is a good God!

By way of illustration, I just bought a new water-sprinkling system for my yard. Now the same grass that

2

took two and a half hours to water manually last year is being watered automatically this year! Last year, I had to drag a hose around and set up sprinklers throughout my yard, but those little sprinklers just didn't do the job adequately. God said to me, "Why don't you just put in a sprinkler system? I can give you the money to do it. Then you can sit out on your front porch in your rocker and watch the sprinkler system spray the yard."

That illustration is just a small example of God's attitude toward us. He cares about us, and He wants us to have good things. God does not want us out dragging around a hose to water a big yard. He wants us to be able to spend our time doing other things. He wants us to be able to sit down and relax and watch a sprinkler system do the work!

Notice what the last part of Jeremiah 29:11 says: **"...to give you an expected end."** That's the way God has set up His program — He has a certain expectation for us. One of those expectations is, He wants us to be financially stable in order to support the Kingdom of God.

In other words, we're going to have to pick up on God's vision for winning souls and furthering the Kingdom. One of the first reasons God wants us to be financially blessed is so we can bless the Kingdom of God.

God Expects Our Cooperation

God has an expectation that we be financially able to support the work of His Kingdom. He also expects our cooperation with Him. In other words, if you are not a tither, and you're not planning to be tither, then you are not a candidate for walking in God's prosperity.

Divine prosperity will never come your way if you are not being a channel God can use to bring financial blessing to His Kingdom. If you think you are going to tap into God's revelation, power, and anointing for prosperity and then be a tightwad with God's money and think only about yourself, you are going to be disappointed, because God is not going to let you in on it. You are not a candidate for divine prosperity.

But if you set your heart to be a channel for God — to be used by Him to put money into churches and ministries that are doing something for Him — then with the proper knowledge, money — financial increase — will not be a problem to you.

There's plenty of money out there in the world, but before we can get people to learn how to receive it, we have to get people qualified to receive it. Then once they are qualified, they must have the knowledge to tap into the prosperity God wants them to have.

Prosperity — Part of the 'Package'

Look at Jeremiah 29:11 in the *New International Version*: "'For I know the plans I have for you,' declares the Lord, 'plans to prosper you and not to harm you, plans to give you hope and a future.'"

God's plan is to prosper us and not to harm us. Did you know that poverty causes harm? Poverty has caused harm to the Church, the Body of Christ. We know from the Scripture that poverty is part of the curse of the Law (*see* Deuteronomy 28:15-68). But Galatians 3:13 says that we are redeemed from the curse of the Law!

We also know from the Word that *sickness* is part of the curse of the Law, but we have learned a few things about our being redeemed from the curse of sickness. We have begun to understand that God wants our bodies well — healed and whole. But I think we have taken hold of the healing message better than we've taken hold of the prosperity aspect of our redemption. Yet healing and prosperity are part of the same package, so to speak.

Spiritual death is also a curse of the Law. But we know that we have eternal life in Christ, so we're not concerned now with the Second Death or eternal death. We know we have been born again and are redeemed from spiritual death.

But we're still short on money! We may as well just face the fact. I mean, there is a lot of *false* prosperity — buying nice suits, ties, shoes, and so forth on credit.

That's not real prosperity. Some Christians drive nice big cars and have nice houses, but both the husband and wife have to work to keep up with all of it. And sometimes one of them has to work *two* jobs. That's not prosperity.

Poverty causes harm, but Jeremiah 29:11 says that God's plan for us is not to harm us. The first part of that verse says, "'For I know the plans I have for you...'" (*NIV*). Now look carefully at the rest of that verse in the *New International Version.*

The next three words say, "...declares the Lord...." So this is a declaration from the Lord!

Then the next part of that verse reads, "'...plans to prosper you and not to harm you. ...'" And the rest of the verse says, "'...plans to give you hope and a future.'"

In Jeremiah, the Lord reveals three things about His plan for us: 1) *to prosper us;* 2) *not to harm us;* and 3) *to give us hope and a future!*

When you really understand what God is saying to you in this verse, life will be different for you. You'll view money differently, and "Money cometh"[1] will start working for you. ("Money cometh" means *a continual supply of money headed in your direction!*)

But, first, you have to be thoroughly convinced that this is what God wants for you. You have to get your mind *on* God's goodness and *off* depending just on your fixed income or your job as your source. By depending on your job or your paycheck, you're limiting an unlimited God and what *He* can do in your life.

God does not have to bless you just through that eight-hour-a-day job of yours. Any morning God wants to, He can deposit into you an "entrepreneur spirit" with a revelation or idea from Him that can turn your life upside down financially! But unless you're open to it, He can't do it.

It doesn't matter what kind of job you have. You might work at a plant or in the school system. You might be a manager, or you might be retired on a fixed income (in the case of the latter, you have to get your mind off "fixed income." You need to "unfix" your fixed-income mentality!).

Right now, you might have yourself set up financially on your check that you get every payday. In other words, that's all the prosperity you have, and that's all you're counting on having. But God wants to change that for you. He doesn't want you to depend on that check for the kind of prosperity He wants you to have. *He* is your source — not your boss or the company you work for!

So get your eyes off your job or your pension to prosper you financially. You're going to be disappointed if you're depending on the world system to help you. You know, all some people get when they retire is a fake designer watch and just enough money to barely get by on! I tell you, this world system is set up to keep you broke. But the *Word* system is set up to cause you to prosper!

Say out loud: "I'm getting off the *world* system and onto the *Word* system *today*!"

Your Destiny Is Prosperity

God's plan for us is to give us hope and a future. Our destiny in Him is prosperity — and I'm talking about *money*! I know there's more to prosperity than money. I know there's such a thing as prospering physically and walking in divine health. There's also such a thing as prosperity in your soul, in your mind, will, and emotions. And there's a prosperity in relationships. There's prosperity for every area of your life. But right now I'm talking about money!

Our destiny is divine prosperity. I want you to look at that word "destiny." It means *to designate, assign,* or *determine in advance.* God has destined us for increase. He has already assigned prosperity to you. God has determined in advance for you to increase. We could say it another way: You are designated by God for prosperity!

Another definition for "destiny" is *the future fixed in advance.* God "fixed" your prosperity on this earth before you ever got here! It is predestined, foreordained, and predetermined that God's children should have more than enough. And as soon as we learn how to cooperate with His Word and get into His flow, money will not be a problem for us; we will be walking in divine prosperity.

What is the basis for God's designating or assigning our prosperity? *A contract.*

Now look at Deuteronomy chapter 8.

> **But thou shalt remember the Lord thy God: for it is he that giveth thee power to get wealth, that he may establish his COVENANT which he sware unto thy fathers, as it is this day.**
> **DEUTERONOMY 8:18**

According to this verse, why does God give us the power to get wealth? To establish His covenant. What is a covenant? A covenant is *a contract or binding agreement.*

God's Covenant Is Everlasting

In the Old Testament, in the lives of Abraham, Isaac, Jacob, and Joseph, we can see that the covenant that God "cut" with Abraham continued down the line and was honored in the lives of Abraham's children and grandchildren. Abraham was the father of Isaac; Isaac was the father of Jacob; and Jacob was the father of Joseph.

So God's covenant with Abraham was honored in the life of Joseph, Abraham's great-grandson. But if you'll read the Book of Genesis, you'll find that many of

Joseph's own brothers were not blessed as Joseph was. In fact, at one time, there was a famine in the land, and they were all but broke; they didn't have any food to eat (*see* Genesis 41:54,56,57; 42:5).

One of the reasons they weren't blessed like Joseph was, they didn't have the right attitude. Did you know that having a wrong attitude will keep money from you and keep you broke? You need to have your attitude straight if you want to receive money from God.

Keep a Right Attitude Toward the Local Church

One attitude many Christians today need to change is their attitude about the local church. God is very interested in the local church. He wants His children fed spiritually and to be raised up in the things of God through the local church. It takes money to run a church and to accomplish all the things God wants a particular local body of believers to accomplish in their city.

But many Christians don't support their local church financially — through tithes and offerings. They are disobeying God, because He told us in His Word to tithe **"...that there may be meat in mine house..."** (Mal. 3:10).

Some people need to change their attitudes about the church where they attend. If they do — if they make that little adjustment in their heart — their church will be blessed, and they will be blessed. When a church is blessed, the congregation will prosper individually. But when a congregation is stingy and tightfisted with their money, it keeps money from coming to them.

Show Honor to Whom Honor Is Due

In every church where I preach, I tell the people to see to it that their pastor and his wife are blessed. When you take care of God's things, He will take care of yours. But not esteeming the office of the pastor is one thing that has been holding some people back concerning money.

You see, you have to put first things first. When you put God first, He will honor and bless you. In other words, when your church is blessed and your pastor has plenty of money in his pocket (without your being critical or concerned about it), then you are in a position for God to give you your increase.

Folks need to release the mentality that the preacher is supposed to be broke. They learned that through certain denominations, and they have the attitude, *The preacher doesn't need very much.*

But the truth is, the higher your pastor goes in finances, the higher you can go too. But if you try to hold him back, the Lord is going to see to it that you are held back too! (Actually, you will be holding *yourself* back because you're not cooperating with God and His Word.)

So if you have ever had a bad attitude toward your pastor — if you have ever held your pastor back financially through your attitude and your lack of giving — you can make a little adjustment in your heart today. You can learn to say and mean from your heart, "Father, I don't care how high my pastor rises; in fact, I *want* him to prosper and be blessed. I don't care what kind of suit or shoes he wears. I don't care what kind of car he drives. Bless him, Lord. As a matter of fact, Lord, from this day forward, I'm going to get in on Your blessings by helping to make sure my pastor is taken care of."

If you have a proper attitude toward your pastor, you'll get in on the prophet's reward (Matt. 10:41). Too many are missing the prophet's reward, because they won't bless the man or woman of God. But there's a reward you can't get any other way than by blessing the man or woman of God; it's called the prophet's reward. In other words, if you bless your pastor, there's a special reward.

When the pastor of a church is giving of his life for the well-being of his flock, the members of that flock need to bless that man or woman of God. The members of that congregation need to make sure they pay their tithes and give offerings so that the church can run properly. And they need to make sure the pastor is prospering.

I know some people don't like hearing that, but it's the truth anyway! But folks who don't want to hear the truth about showing honor to whom honor is due and esteeming their pastor are going to either stay broke, or they're not going to increase and rise to the level financially that God wants them to. (*See* Philippians 4:15-19.)

When You Cooperate With God, It's Easy To Have Plenty of Money!

One of the things the Holy Spirit has taught me about money is that it's the easiest thing in the world to have plenty of it!

I said, it's very easy to have plenty of money. I say that based on the Word, on what the Holy Spirit has taught me, and on my own experiences in this area. Not only have I experienced some great financial breakthroughs and blessings, but I have great expectation for the future, not just for me and my family and ministry, but for you, too, for the Body of Christ!

It's easy to have plenty of money. All you have to do is obey Isaiah 1:19 and Malachi 3:10.

If ye be willing and obedient, ye shall eat the good of the land.

ISAIAH 1:19

Bring ye all the tithes into the storehouse, that there may be meat in mine house, and prove me now herewith, saith the Lord of hosts, if I will not open you the windows of heaven, and pour you out a blessing, that there shall not be room enough to receive it.

MALACHI 3:10

Many people have been tithing and not receiving their return because they're not walking by faith and taking God at His Word, or they're not being obedient in some other area, such as in their attitude toward the things of God and toward His people, especially His ministers.

Others aren't being blessed because they give to the Kingdom of God grudgingly. They're not giving freely or cheerfully (2 Cor. 9:7). They're giving with certain strings attached. They want to get in the basket with their money when the offering basket goes by! Do you know what I mean by that? I mean, they won't allow the people who have been appointed to lead that church or ministry to take care of the offerings that are received. They are always questioning and wondering, *What's going on with the money?* and they're always suspicious.

But when you give offerings, you are doing what God told you to do in His Word. So after you give, the rest of the responsibility is on God's people who are handling that money. You've obeyed God, and He's the One who's going to cause finances to come back to you because you've given with a good heart and a right attitude.

God wants His children to have plenty, plenty, *plenty* of money! He wants His children to have all their bills paid with money left over — with an ample supply. But God's covenant of prosperity is also a covenant of *obedience* and *cooperation*.

Are You in *Covenant* or *Covetousness?*

We need to look briefly at the difference between "covenant" and "covetousness," because if you are coveting money, you are never going to have any! These two words, "covenant" and "covetousness," will determine how far you are going to go in your finances.

We know from reading Deuteronomy 8:18 that we have a money covenant with God. We are to remember Him with our finances, because He is the one who gives us the power to get wealth so that He can establish His covenant with us upon the earth.

But what about that word "covetousness"? What does it mean to be covetous? Well, if you are not a tither — if you are not giving God the tithe or ten percent of your income according to Malachi 3:10 — you are being covetous. In other words, you are taking something that belongs to someone else, and that "someone else" is God!

> Will a man rob God? Yet ye have robbed me. But ye say, Wherein have we robbed thee? In tithes and offerings.
> Ye are cursed with a curse: for ye have robbed me, even this whole nation.
> Bring ye all the tithes into the storehouse, that there may be meat in mine house, and prove me now herewith, saith the Lord of hosts, if I will not open you the windows of heaven, and pour you out

a blessing, that there shall not be room enough to receive it.

MALACHI 3:8-10

So, you see, according to this passage of Scripture, if you are not a tither, you are stealing from God, and the Word says, **"Ye are cursed with a curse..."** (v. 9).

Well, what does it mean to be "cursed with a curse"? It means you might get your hands on a few dollars in life, but you won't be blessed. For example, you might not be well enough to enjoy that money.

Let me explain that. If you are not tithing according to God's Word, then you are disobeying God's Word. Well, if you aren't living in line with the Word, then you are in cahoots, so to speak, with Satan through your disobedience. Now Satan will let you have some money, but if you give place to him, he might give you something else too! He might give you some sickness and disease to go along with that money!

You have to be very careful to understand the difference between covenant and covetousness. Covetousness is how the devil has tripped up some people. Satan is the god of covetousness; God is the God of covenant!

The way you determine whether you're in covenant or covetousness is simple. If you are obeying God in your finances, then you are in covenant. But if you are tight, selfish, and stingy, and you're always going after money, then you are in covetousness.

Money in Itself Is Neither Evil Nor Good

Let me explain something about another scripture than can help us determine where we're at when it comes to walking in God's divine plan for finances.

> **For the love of money is the root of all evil: which while some coveted after, they have erred from the faith, and pierced themselves through with many sorrows.**
>
> **1 TIMOTHY 6:10**

You know, Satan has preached this verse and has used it more than just about anyone! He even uses preachers who are what I call "Bible illiterates" to hold people back from prospering. They get in their pulpits and preach to people that it's not God's will for them to have anything.

I've seen it happen. When people start to rise up in their finances and get a nice home or a nice car, these preachers start preaching at them. A husband and wife could go to church dressed really nice, and instead of introducing himself to them and making friends with them, the preacher will get his old dumb self behind the pulpit and start preaching against them, putting down the message of prosperity.

Preachers who do that don't know any better — they are Bible illiterates. Many of them have used First Timothy 6:10 to try to prove that money is evil and that God doesn't want you to have any of it.

First of all, let me get it straight who this verse in First Timothy is talking about. Timothy was not talking to Christians who love the Lord and want to obey Him. And he's not necessarily just talking to the rich, either.

First Timothy 6:10 says, **"For the LOVE OF MONEY is the root of all evil: which while some coveted after, they have erred from the faith, and pierced themselves through with many sorrows."**

You know, poor people can love money as much as some rich people love it. And the Bible says it's the *love* of money that's evil. Money in itself is not evil. Money is what you make it. In other words, it's people's attitudes about money that can be evil.

You can go to any jailhouse and find people who were locked up because they loved money and robbed someone. And they robbed someone because they were broke! Don't misunderstand me. Being broke is no excuse to rob someone. But people who have money don't usually rob other people! So, you see, a broke person could love money as much as a rich person could. And it's the *love* of money that's evil, not money itself.

Now read First Timothy 6:10 again: **"For the love of money is the root of all evil: which while SOME COVETED AFTER, they have erred from the faith, and pierced themselves through with many sorrows."**

Three Bible Examples of Covetousness

The rich farmer in Luke chapter 12, the rich young ruler in Mark chapter 10 and Luke chapter 18, and the rich man and Lazarus in Luke chapter 16 all show examples of covetousness. Satan has used those stories to tell us that riches are bad, but you have to study the context of the messages to know why each situation turned out badly.

For example, the rich young ruler didn't have money — money had *him*! And the rich farmer prospered, but he didn't recognize the One who caused him to prosper.

The rich man who didn't have mercy on Lazarus also forgot to give God credit for his prosperity. He didn't do the right things with his money. The Bible says he **"...was clothed in purple and fine linen, and fared sumptuously every day"** (Luke 16:19). But he ignored Lazarus' plea for mercy. He didn't give glory to God with his money.

That's why each of those three people were rich fools. They loved money, and it became evil to them.

Do you understand now why money in itself is neither evil nor good?

You remember I told you how to tell if you were in covenant or in covetousness? A person who is just going after money is covetous. But for the person who obeys

God and follows Him, money *cometh*! Money comes after *him*!

How To Get Money To Follow You!

You see, when you're in covenant with God concerning finances, money comes after you; you don't go after money. Psalm 23:6 says, **"Surely goodness and mercy shall FOLLOW me all the days of my life: and I will dwell in the house of the Lord for ever."**

When you get this revelation clear about God's will for you concerning finances, then not only will goodness and mercy follow you, *money* will follow you all the days of your life! Why? Because you've humbled yourself before God — you've proved yourself and you've passed the test. You understand that man does not live by bread alone but by every word that proceedeth from the mouth of God (Matthew 4:4; Luke 4:4). You know where prosperity comes from — from God's Word. Your heart is straight with God; He knows what is in your heart, and He can trust you with money.

Some people need to let God work in their hearts concerning obedience in their finances. Then He can put them in position and in the right "socket" to receive finances from God. Look again at Isaiah 1:19.

> **If ye be willing and obedient, ye shall eat the good of the land.**
>
> **ISAIAH 1:19**

This verse says that if you are willing and obedient, you shall eat the good of the land. You know, some people try to put all kinds of interpretations on this verse and relegate it to just eating good food! But "the good of the land" is referring to the things you need and desire in every area of your life! God is saying, "If ye be willing and obedient, I'll see that you get the things you need and want"!

If we are willing and obedient and understand what God wants to do for us in our finances, we will not struggle about money anymore.

Look again at Deuteronomy 8:18, because it is a companion verse to Isaiah 1:19. These verses are "qualifying" verses to help us get into position so that money can be loosed to us and we can increase financially. God said, **"But thou shalt remember the Lord thy God: for it is he that giveth thee POWER to get wealth, that he may establish his covenant which he sware unto thy fathers, as it is this day."**

God's Word Is His Power

First, notice the phrase concerning the covenant: **"...which he sware unto thy fathers...."** The Lord gave His Word on it!

Do you understand that the Lord's Word is good? When He says something, you know you can depend on it, because His Word is good. I like the verse that says, "For with God nothing is ever impossible and no word from God shall be without power or impossible of fulfillment" (Luke 1:37 *Amp.*) In other words, God's Word contains enough power within itself to cause it to come to pass!

God's Word doesn't need help having any more power than it already has. God's words are containers; they contain the ability of God to cause the natural to become *supernatural* and impossibilities *possible*!

I'm talking about having a correct attitude and mindset about money. In order to fulfill our destiny to increase financially, you have to be fully persuaded and convinced that God's plan is to prosper you and that prosperity is the divine will of God for your life. Then you have to learn how to think about money so that you can cooperate with God by having a right attitude and by receiving His blessing by faith. You are destined for increase!

---

¹For an in-depth study of the subject "Money cometh," see Dr. Thompson's book *Money Cometh to the Body of Christ!*

A couple of years ago, I began teaching heavily on the subject of prosperity because God gave me a commission to teach it to the Body of Christ. God doesn't want His children broke and barely getting by, and yet many of them are living beneath their rights and privileges in Christ.

God wants all of His children to have plenty of money. He wants them to be "loaded" and have "good measure, pressed down, shaken together, and running over" (Luke 6:38) in their finances!

If you're broke, God doesn't want you to be broke anymore! If you're prospering, God wants more for you! He wants you to prosper more and to take even more territory in the realm of finances. God wants you to give more to His Kingdom as you receive more — as you possess what He wants you to have.

I want to teach you how to take authority over money and make money obey you. Money has no authority in itself; it must do what you tell it to do. So I'm going to show you from the Scriptures how to take authority over money and "loose" it so you can get it flowing in your life.

Giving and Receiving:
Putting First Things First

One of the first things you have to do in order to take authority over money is to understand that there are two sides to the principle of giving and receiving. In other words, before you can take authority over *receiving*, you have to take authority over your *giving*.

Many people are trying to take authority over receiving first. They'll confess, "Bless God, I'm prosperous. I'm the head and not the tail" (Deut. 28:13). But, no, they need to take authority over their *giving* first.

When you take authority over your giving — when you get to the place where you're not letting your money rule you, and you're obeying the Spirit of God in giving — *then* you can turn to the receiving end of "giving and receiving" and tell *receiving* what you want to receive!

More and More!

Look at Psalm 115 at some verses that give us insight about what God has intended for us — what He has wanted to do for us all along.

He will bless them that fear the Lord, both small and great.

The Lord shall increase you more and more, you and your children.

PSALM 115:13,14

Verse 13 says, **"He will bless them that fear the Lord, both small and great."** You see, from the aspect of God's desire to bless His children, He covers everyone — the small and the great! Now notice verse 14: **"The Lord shall increase you MORE AND MORE, you and your children."**

I like those three words *"more and more."* It would do you good to say them out loud: "The Lord shall increase me *more and more!*"

Now why would the Lord increase you more and more? So you can increase your giving! Then as you increase your giving, He can in turn increase you more and more — *so that you can increase your giving, so that He can increase you more and more!*

Do you see how that works? When you put first things first and take authority over your *giving*, God will help you take authority over your *receiving*, and He will increase you more and more!

"That sounds good," you might say. "I want to take authority over receiving and increase more and more in my finances. I know I need to take authority over my giving first, but just how am I to do that?"

It's very simple. You take authority over your giving by remembering the Lord in your giving — by giving to Him and His work because you know that every good thing you have in life, you have it because of Him.

Remember the Lord

We looked briefly at Deuteronomy 8:18 in Chapter 1. Let's look again at this important scripture.

But thou shalt REMEMBER THE LORD THY GOD: for it is he that giveth thee power to get wealth, that he may establish his covenant which he sware unto thy fathers, as it is this day.

DEUTERONOMY 8:18

Deuteronomy 8 is talking about God's blessing — and that blessing includes money! Verse 18 says, **"But thou shalt REMEMBER the Lord thy God...."**

Actually, if you look at that statement clearly, you can see that one of the main ways to remember God is by your giving — by your taking authority over giving! That's one of the main ways that God "finds you out." (People like to remember God in prayer and by quoting their favorite scripture, but for the purpose of this book, I'm talking about remembering God with your *money*.)

Why do we need to remember God with our money? Because there are lost people in this world. The Son of

Man came to seek and to save that which was lost (Luke 19:10). We need money to get this Gospel out so the lost can be saved.

The Bible also tells us in First John 3:8, **"...For this purpose the Son of God was manifested, that he might destroy the works of the devil."** And then Jesus said, **"...I am come that they might have life, and that they might have it more abundantly"** (John 10:10).

These scriptures tell us things that God is concerned about: 1) *seeking and saving that which is lost*; 2) *destroying the works of the devil in people's lives*; and 3) *seeing that His people have life and have it more abundantly.*

God is concerned about all three of these things, and it takes money to carry them out! It takes money to preach the Gospel, to get the lost saved, and to destroy the works of the devil in people's lives. It takes money to preach the Gospel so people can have a more abundant life!

Therefore, since we know the things God is concerned about and that it takes money to do these things, we know that your having plenty of money is the will of God too! (So if you are not prospering and living the abundant life financially, then in one sense, you are not living in God's will. You're out of the will of God in the area of prosperity — in the area of having what He wants you to have.)

Now I'm going show you how the Lord checks you out — how He checks the attitude of your heart — because anyone can raise his hands and say, "Lord, how I love You." But it takes more than just raising your hands, talking about how much you love the Lord, and coming to church with a big Bible that's marked up to prove that you love Him!

As I said, one of the main ways God checks you out is by your giving. In other words, if you can't separate yourself from money, especially in the area of tithing (Mal. 3:10), you don't really love God or trust Him. If you can't remember the Lord your God with your money, you don't believe that God is who He says He is. But God is bigger than any one of us can ever think! And He has everything we need and more besides.

So we know that the first step to taking authority over money — over your giving and your receiving — is to remember the Lord with your money.

I want to prove further that God checks you out by your giving. Look at Mark chapter 12.

> **And Jesus sat over against the treasury, and BEHELD HOW THE PEOPLE CAST MONEY INTO THE TREASURY: and many that were rich cast in much.**
> **And there came a certain poor widow, and she threw in two mites, which make a farthing.**

**And he called unto him his disciples, and saith
unto them, Verily I say unto you, That this poor
widow hath cast more in, than all they which have
cast into the treasury:
For all they did cast in of their abundance; but she
of her want did cast in all that she had, even all her
living.**

MARK 12:41-44

Many people have heard ministers preach on these
verses about the widow who gave more than everyone
else because she gave all that she had. But I see
something else in these verses. Jesus was not sitting "over
against the treasury" watching those who were in prayer!
He was not watching those who were talking about how
much they loved the Lord. And He wasn't watching
anyone singing or laying hands on the sick. No, Jesus was
watching those who were giving money!

Your Money Is Your 'Measuring Stick'!

Actually, your money and how you give it to the Lord
and His work is your measuring stick, so to speak, of how
much you love God. Some people don't want to touch the
subject of money in connection with how much they love
God. They want to stay in a "spiritual" frame of mind
when they talk about loving the Lord.

But the measuring stick of your love for God is that
which you have sweated and worked for — whether you

can give it freely and cheerfully. (If you measure high on the stick, that means you give your money to God freely and cheerfully because you know He caused you to have that job or source of income in the first place!)

The Lord judges by your wallet and your pocketbook to know whether or not you really love Him! I can prove that even further. The Bible says in Luke 12:34, **"For where your treasure is, there will your heart be also."** So if our heart is really in a ministry or in the work of God, our treasure will be there also!

Jesus watches our giving. And I believe that in our giving, Jesus finds out who we really are. You know, people like to give testimonies, talk about the things of God, and make confessions. And those things are good. But the Lord is not only present when you're *talking*, He's present when you're *giving* too! If God were in the church office at the church you attend and was looking at the records of your giving, He might be saying something like, "I want to see how much he really loves Me." And He could tell how much you love Him by your money — by how well you've been giving!

Now really super-spiritual folks will tell you that God is not concerned about your money and how much you give. But, yes, He is. And do you know why? Because if you're not giving properly — if you're not tithing and giving offerings — you are holding God back from doing for you what He wants to do! God wants to be a good

Father to you in the area of finances. And if you're giving properly, you're giving Him the right to do it!

There is no shortage of money; there's plenty of money in this world. For instance, I stayed in a hotel in Las Vegas, where I preached a meeting, that had been purchased for $30,000,000, and the owners paid cash for it. There were slot machines everywhere in that hotel, and people played those machines all night long. Thousands of dollars exchanged hands in that place every day.

So there's no shortage of money in this world. It's just that the Church has to take its place so that believers can take back what rightfully belongs to them. They'll have to get their mind renewed and their attitude straight about money. Then they'll be able to prosper more and more.

You Are Money's Master!

In this book, I'm going to show you how to make money obey you. Did you know that you can talk to money, and money will have to turn and come your way?

God has shown me personally how to master money. There was a time when my wife Carolyn and I couldn't give $10 in an offering over and beyond our tithes. But now we can give thousands, and it's because of some of the principles from God's Word that I'm going to teach you in this book.

And when they [Jesus and the disciples] **were come
to Capernaum, they that received tribute money
came to Peter, and said, Doth not your master pay
tribute?
He saith, Yes. And when he was come into the
house, Jesus prevented him, saying, What thinkest
thou, Simon? of whom do the kings of the earth
take custom or tribute? of their own children, or of
strangers?
Peter saith unto him, Of strangers. Jesus saith unto
him, Then are the children free.
Notwithstanding, lest we should offend them, go
thou to the sea, and cast an hook, and take up the
fish that first cometh up; and when thou hast
opened his mouth, thou shalt find a piece of
money: that take, and give unto them for me and
thee.**

MATTHEW 17:24-27

Look at verse 27. Jesus told Peter to do something out
of the ordinary. Jesus told him, **"...go thou to the sea,
and cast an hook, and take up the fish that first cometh
up; and when thou hast opened his mouth, thou shalt
find a piece of money: that take, and give unto them for
me and thee."**

Now Peter was a professional fisherman, yet I'm sure
he'd never heard of doing anything like that before! But
when you hook your money up with Jesus, anything can

happen! When you hook your finances up with Jesus, your finances move out of the ordinary into the *extra*ordinary! God will grant you divine favor and open up certain opportunities to you — *doors* of opportunity. Someone else may have tried to go through those same doors but couldn't get through. Yet you come along — in the plan and will of God — and the doors swing wide open for you!

The Bible says, **"If ye be willing and obedient, ye shall eat the good of the land"** (Isa. 1:19). If you are willing and obedient to God, He will open a channel for you to get through. God will find favor for you when you take authority over your giving by sowing finances into the Kingdom of God in obedience to Him. When you take authority over your giving, God must help you take authority over your receiving!

God *wants* to work supernaturally in our finances. He wants us to be out of debt. He does not want us ever to be broke another day in our life. God wants us to have all the finances we need to get the job done of preaching the Gospel across the world. Then He wants us to have enough left over to enjoy life. Living from paycheck to paycheck is "hell" on earth! God did not mean for His children to live from paycheck to paycheck. He wants us to have an abundant supply — *more and more*! He wants to increase us financially.

We've already seen that money in itself is neither evil nor good. Some people like to "quote" that text in First

Timothy, saying, "Money is the root of all evil." But they are misquoting that verse, because First Timothy 6:10 says, **"For the LOVE OF MONEY is the root of all evil..."**! It is the love of money that's evil, not money itself. (And the lack of money is evil, too, because it's not of God!)

First Timothy 6:10 doesn't apply to those who are taking authority over their giving. Those people who are putting God first in every area, including their finances, don't love money. One of the signs of someone who loves money is, he is not a tither and a giver. He loves money more than he loves God.

Look again at Matthew 17:27: **"...go thou to the sea, and cast an hook, and take up the fish that first cometh up; and when thou hast opened his mouth, thou shalt find a piece of money: that take, and give unto them for me and thee."**

Once as I was studying this passage of Scripture in Matthew 17, God brought something else to my attention: God can change a nonproductive business into a productive one *supernaturally* if the proprietor will give Him first priority!

As I said, Peter was a professional fisherman. Yet he'd never opened a fish's mouth to get money to pay taxes until Jesus told him to do it. Jesus even told him where to find the fish! That incident was not ordinary — it was *extra*ordinary! God supernaturally prospered Peter because Peter put God first and gave Him first priority in his life.

So you see, even if a business is failing, if the owner will get God to moving in his finances, things will turn around and happen for him supernaturally. And the way he gets God involved in his finances is by giving.

When God Tells You To Give, Just Do It!

One time a certain preacher pulled up behind my car in his brand-new Mercedes Benz automobile. I happened to know that this minister was building a new house. When he drove up behind me, the Spirit of God told me, "You give him five hundred dollars."

Now what would have been your argument with God? Number one, here this man was, driving a new Mercedes. And, number two, he was getting ready to move into a brand-new house. But when God said to me, "You give him five hundred dollars," I said, "Yes, God. I'll do it." I called my wife and gave her the man's name and told her to write him a check.

Within about three weeks of giving that money, I came into possession of $11,500! God told me, "The seed you planted into that minister's life is where that money came from that you received." I knew it was true, not only because He told me, but because the first $1,500 of that $11,500 came to me in three $500 increments! God made sure that I knew where that money came from (and why it came)!

Then a certain young minister came to me and told me how much he loved me and appreciated my ministry. He told me that he'd greatly benefited from the teaching he'd received from me, and the Lord had opened up many opportunities to him. He said, "I want to give you this check..." He paused, and then he said, "...for ten thousand dollars." When he said that, my knees sort of buckled under me! I had to tell my knees, "Straighten up!"

Here's something I want you to see. This minister was young; he was just starting out in life. He wasn't like some big-name minister who could easily give a $10,000 offering without batting an eye. But that's how money often comes — through unlikely sources.

God wants you to have money. And He will put it on people's hearts to bless you. Why? Because of your seed in the ground — because you've continually sown seed by your giving. If you take authority over your giving, God will take authority over your receiving for you!

Giving: Over and Beyond the Tithe

Through your giving — through your remembering the Lord — you can permit Jesus to function supernaturally in your finances. A lack of money and never having enough has been lording it over the people of God too long. But there's a new breed of believers rising up who are taking authority over money.

Say this out loud: "I am taking authority over money *now!*"

You can take authority over money; I'm going to show you how. (When I preach about money, some people look at me like they just ate a sour lemon; they get *upset*! But they're going to get left behind if they don't become teachable and listen to what God has to say about money.)

Look at Deuteronomy 8:18 again: **"But thou shalt remember the Lord thy God: for it is he that giveth thee power to get wealth, that he may establish his covenant which he sware unto thy fathers, as it is this day."** One way of remembering that God has been good to you is to give back to Him what's due and then over and beyond what's due.

As I said, some people spiritualize this verse and say, "Well, I remember the Lord. I love Him. I prayed this morning. I went to church last week, and I'm going again this week."

No, one of the biggest ways to remember the Lord is to remember to pay tithes and then to give big! I like something a certain minister said. He said, in effect, "The *tithe* is something you *owe*. The *offering* is a seed you *sow*." I also like what one sister said in giving her testimony. She said that when she started tithing, she had two things working for her: *security* and *confidence*. She was secure in her knowledge of the Word and had confidence that God would do what He said in His Word He would do. She was remembering the Lord.

You see, no economic crisis reported on television or in the newspaper ever bothers me, because I'm not on the world system. I'm on the *Word* system, and I can't go down unless *Jesus* goes down! And Jesus is not going down. Therefore, I am full of confidence about money. I can't worry about how I'm going to make it. I know that I already have it made, because I'm walking in God's divine plan, and He is divinely supplying all of my needs. When others can't get money, I'll have it.

Some people say, "It's easy for you to talk about prosperity, because you're a preacher." But I could take you to "Preacher Row" and show you many broke preachers who don't have any confidence in God concerning money. They have congregations that don't have any confidence, either, and they keep those preachers broke! They have deacon boards that have meetings every week to discuss how broke they can keep the preacher!

So don't say, "Well, Brother Thompson is blessed because he's a preacher." I know why I'm blessed. It's not because I'm a preacher. I'm blessed because I'm in the divine will of God, and you can be blessed in the divine will of God too.

We're Eagles, Not Chickens!

You can give the devil a black eye by keeping yourself in God's plan and will for your life and by living in line with the Word that shows you who you are in Christ.

Many Christians don't realize who they are or what belongs to them in Christ. They are like chickens in a chicken yard. They just pick up bugs, worms, and scraps, because they don't really know what belongs to them. But the Bible says, **"Thou preparest a table before me in the presence of mine enemies. . . "** (Ps. 23:5). Those Christians should be eating from the Lord's table, not picking up worms and just barely getting by! They're "picking" like a chicken when they should be flying like an eagle!

We should be flying with the eagles in our finances! God has provided for us to be eagles, not chickens!

Make that confession: "I'm flying like an eagle in my finances! Money cometh to *me — now!*

God Gives Money Power!

Look again at Deuteronomy 8:18: **"But thou shalt remember the Lord thy God: for it is he that giveth thee POWER to get wealth, that he may establish his covenant which he sware unto thy fathers, as it is this day."**

Notice that word "power" in this verse. You see, the Lord is not going to give you *wealth*. He gives you *power* to get wealth. Through His Word and His financial plan, He gives you the power to get wealth. He's not going to give you the wealth, because He's already provided you with wealth in His redemptive plan. There is no limit to the things God wants you to have in life, but you have to take hold of the power He gives in order to obtain them.

Would you like to take authority over money — over your giving *and* your receiving — so that you can have more money and enjoy it like God wants you to? If you're going to take authority over money and make money obey you, you're going to have to do it according to the Word. You're going to have to love the Word of God and give it first place in your life.

> I love them that LOVE ME; and those that SEEK ME EARLY shall find me.
> RICHES AND HONOUR ARE WITH ME; yea, durable riches and righteousness.
> My fruit is better than gold, yea, than fine gold; and my REVENUE than choice silver.
> I lead in the way of righteousness, in the midst of the paths of judgment:
> That I may CAUSE THOSE THAT LOVE ME TO INHERIT SUBSTANCE; and I will FILL THEIR TREASURES.
>
> **PROVERBS 8:17-21**

First, look at verse 19: **"My fruit is better than gold, yea, than fine gold; and my REVENUE than choice silver."** That word "revenue" is bank talk! That's talking about money! Now look at verse 21: **"That I may cause those that love me TO INHERIT SUBSTANCE; and I WILL FILL THEIR TREASURES."**

Would you like to inherit substance? Would you like to have your treasures filled? Your giving is the first step. You must give in faith — you must give because you believe what the Word of God says about giving and receiving. Then you need to add something to your giving: You need to add your confession. Once you are giving in line with the Word, you have the right to take authority over the receiving end of "giving and receiving" by commanding money to come to you — by loosing it unto yourself. And money must obey you!

I've been talking about how much God wants you to increase financially. Remember, I said that prosperity is not going to be automatic or come overnight, but there are some things we can do to cooperate with God in faith and cause money to be loosed unto us. All the money we'll ever need is here; there's *plenty* of money here on the earth. But we have to find out how to loose it and get it to come to us.

One way I said we could do that is through our faith and our obedience. We have to first believe that it's the will of God that we prosper and increase financially, and we have to be tithers and givers to the Lord's work. I can't tell you how many times I've given money to someone, and soon thereafter, here comes someone giving *me* money! It happens all the time.

Another thing you have to remember is, you can't be ready for a big harvest if you haven't sown big. Second Corinthians 9:6 says, **"But this I say, He which soweth sparingly shall reap also sparingly; and he which soweth bountifully shall reap also bountifully."** In other words, the degree to which you take authority over your giving is the degree to which you can take authority over your receiving.

Let me show you something about loosing money from a verse you're probably already familiar with.

> **Verily I say unto you, Whatsoever ye shall BIND on earth shall be BOUND in heaven: and whatsoever ye shall LOOSE on earth shall be LOOSED in heaven.**
>
> **MATTHEW 18:18**

First, notice that word "shall." Whatsoever you shall bind on earth shall be bound in Heaven, and whatsoever you shall loose on earth shall be loosed in Heaven.

Now I want to concentrate on the last part of that verse: "...**whatsoever ye shall loose on earth shall be loosed in heaven.**"

What does "loose" mean? It means *to let go; untie; release;* and *set free.* Through the knowledge of God's Word and His will concerning your prosperity, you can *bind* poverty and lack in your life and *loose* or *release* divine prosperity and abundance!

Notice another word in that verse: *whatsoever.* What does "whatsoever" mean? It means *anything.* Well, does "anything" include money? Certainly, it does. Jesus said, "...**WHATSOEVER ye shall loose on earth shall be loosed in heaven**" (Matt. 18:18). It doesn't make any difference what it is — if you loose it, Jesus said, "*I'll* loose it."

Do you realize what Jesus is saying? First, He is saying, in effect, "Whatever is loosed in your life is going to be loosed because *you're* doing the loosing, not Me. It's not up to Me to loose it first. *You* are to 'call the shots.' But when you loose something according to My Word, no one can stop it from being loosed"!

When I talk about binding and loosing according to Matthew 18:18, I'm not talking about some formula. I'm talking about faith. It takes faith to use this verse. Mere talk or "lip service" is not enough.

Don't Ask for More Faith — Use the Faith You Already Have!

Let's look at Luke's Gospel at something else about faith.

> **And the apostles said unto the Lord, Increase our faith.**
> **And the Lord said, If ye had faith as a grain of mustard seed, ye might say unto this sycamine tree, Be thou plucked up by the root, and be thou planted in the sea; and it should obey you.**
> **LUKE 17:5,6**

When the apostles asked the Lord in verse 5 to increase their faith, Jesus answered them, saying, in effect, "You don't need more faith. You just need to use the faith you already have." He said, **"...If ye had faith as a grain of mustard seed, ye might say unto this sycamine tree, Be thou plucked up by the root, and be thou planted in the sea; and it should obey you."**

I want you to see the last statement in that verse. Jesus was not talking just about a sycamine tree. He was giving a physical illustration using objects that were probably in the vicinity of where He was at the time.

What was Jesus referring to in regard to the sycamine tree. He was talking about faith's ability. He said that when you speak to something in faith, whatever you speak to must obey you.

Luke 17:6 could easily read, "If you say to money, 'Be plucked up and come over to my house,' it should obey you." You remember Jesus said over in Matthew 18:18, **"Verily I say unto you, WHATSOEVER ye shall bind on earth shall be bound in heaven: and WHATSOEVER ye shall loose on earth shall be loosed in heaven."**

Going back to Luke 17:6 again, Jesus said, **"...If ye had faith as a grain of mustard seed, ye might say unto this sycamine tree, Be thou plucked up by the root, and be thou planted in the sea; and it should obey you."** Jesus was saying, "If you have faith just as a grain of mustard seed, you could do this. And you already have that much faith"!

When I was still in my old denomination, we preachers in my circles used to talk about the size of the mustard seed. But Jesus wasn't really emphasizing the *size* of a mustard seed as much as He was emphasizing the *power* of a mustard seed! In other words, that mustard seed had the power within itself to cause a big mustard plant to grow, *but it had to be planted in order to be effective!*

In other words, a seed laying on top of the ground can't get the job done. It must be put in the soil. In the same way, your faith has to be planted or spoken, and you have to continue to speak to it to get the job done. Then whatever it is you are using your faith on according to the Word must obey you. Jesus said that whatsoever you loose on earth shall be loosed in Heaven, and Jesus is not a liar.

Our minds have told us that having money is a difficult thing. Having money is not difficult, but we have to change our thinking about money. (Actually, it's more difficult *not* to have money!)

When I talk about the subject of "Money, thou art loosed," what I want you to see is that the Spirit of God is saying that we have the ability to loose all the money that we need or desire in life by our obedience and by speaking the Word with confidence and full assurance.

> **For our gospel came not unto you in word only, but also in power, and in the Holy Ghost, and in MUCH ASSURANCE; as ye know what manner of men we were among you for your sake.**
>
> **1 THESSALONIANS 1:5**

Many people have been making positive, even Word-based, confessions about money, but there's more to it than that. You have to make your confession in the spirit of faith, which believes and speaks (2 Cor. 4:13). When you know with "much assurance" that money must obey you as the sycamine tree obeyed Jesus in Luke 17, you will begin to see results in your finances.

Look at the first part of First Thessalonians 1:5: **"For our gospel came not unto you in word only...."** Paul didn't say the Gospel didn't come in words; he said it didn't come in words *only*. So when you're talking about loosing money or about any Bible subject, you can't teach it or learn it in words only. You have to have the truth down in your spirit. Then it will become power unto you for whatever it is you need.

That's why when I preach, I exhort people to listen with the intent to receive. The Bible says, **"... receive with meekness the engrafted word, which is able to save your souls"** (James 1:21). That's talking about being teachable.

I often teach about the men who gathered around David in First Samuel 22. It says they were in distress, in debt, and in discontentment (v. 2). David was a man who had the spirit of faith, and I believe that when David had meetings with his men, he spoke to them, not just in words, but in power, in the Holy Ghost, and in much assurance. And I can just see one of those men who was broke standing up one day and saying, "I've got it! What you're saying is catching on; it's catching hold of me. I believe I can do what you're telling us we can do."

It's the same way today when people listen with the intent to receive from men of God who have that same spirit of faith. After awhile, they'll say, "I've got it! Glory to God! This man of God got to the place where he could give to the church twenty thousand dollars above his tithe. I believe I'm going to get there too."

God does not have any "pets" or favorites. He doesn't just want ten or fifteen people in the Body of Christ to get rich and make it big in life. No, God honors anyone who will say, "Lord, I believe what I've been hearing from Your Word. It's in my heart; I'm taking it as my own."

Don't Wait for Someone Else To Do It for You — You Take By Faith What Belongs to You!

Sometimes believers get all "hyped up" at a meeting because a corporate or collective anointing is present. But in the day-to-day world where the rubber meets the road, so to speak, it all comes down to what you believe individually. Jesus said, **"... If YE had faith as a grain of mustard seed, YE might say unto this sycamine tree, Be thou plucked up by the root, and be thou planted in the sea; and it should obey YOU"** (Luke 17:6). Jesus also said, **"... Whatsoever YE shall bind on earth shall be bound in heaven: and whatsoever YE shall loose on earth shall be loosed in heaven"** (Matt. 18:18).

A Dynamic Trio: Obedience, Faith, and a Pure Heart

Going back to my statement, "If you take authority over your giving, you can take authority over your receiving," all of these things — a right motive, faith, and sowing seed — work together. In other words, it's not just your right motive that will cause money and divine prosperity to be loosed unto you. And it's not just faith, either. You could speak the Word in faith all you want, but if there are no works, such as giving, behind your faith, your faith will be unproductive. Then there are those who give and give, but they don't know what belongs to them in Christ. They don't have the revelation that prosperity is their right; therefore, they don't stand their ground in faith about it, and prosperity often passes them by.

But all of these things working together can produce wealth in your life. God wants to you be rich, with all your needs liberally supplied and having enough to give to "every good work" (Phil. 4:19; 2 Cor. 9:8). As I said before, God doesn't want just a few to "make it." He wants every Christian to rise up and, independent of circumstances, appropriate the prosperity that belongs to him.

But it is your choice. God is not going to *make* you receive wealth. Often, believers miss it because they think money is just going to "fall" on them without any effort on their part. Or they make excuses, such as, "Well, you know So-and-so was born into a rich family; that's why he's rich. But *I* could never be rich." Then others think they are waiting on God, when, really, He is waiting on them!

But you don't have to wait to walk in divine prosperity. Prosperity can begin today for you, in your spirit. You just have to stick with it and not become moved by the circumstances around you, such as debt, lay-offs at your job, or the economy. God wants you to begin today to see yourself as prosperous and as having the best — and not just at Christmastime! He wants you to become a master over money. But in order to do that, the Word on the subject of money has to be real to you.

Often, folks have memorized scriptures, but that is not enough. They've memorized verses, but they haven't spent enough time with those verses for them to become real — for those verses to become Spirit and life (John 6:63) — to their spirit.

Another trap some believers fall into is allowing their statements that are supposed to be statements of faith to become just slogans. For example, you could say, "God said it, I believe it, and that settles it," and you could mean that from your heart. Or you could say it without it meaning a thing to you. It might just sound good and right, so you say it.

Let's look at a passage of Scripture that talks about binding and loosing from a different aspect — from the aspect of the covenant.

And he [Jesus] was teaching in one of the synagogues on the sabbath.

And, behold, there was a woman which had a spirit of infirmity eighteen years, and was bowed together, and could in no wise lift up herself.

And when Jesus saw her, he called her to him, and said unto her, Woman, THOU ART LOOSED from thine infirmity.

And he laid his hands on her: and immediately she was made straight, and glorified God.

And the ruler of the synagogue answered with indignation, because that Jesus had healed on the sabbath day, and said unto the people, There are six days in which men ought to work: in them therefore come and be healed, and not on the sabbath day.

The Lord then answered him, and said, Thou hypocrite, doth not each one of you on the sabbath loose his ox or his ass from the stall, and lead him away to watering?

And ought not this woman, being a daughter of Abraham, whom Satan hath bound, lo, these eighteen years, be LOOSED from this bond on the sabbath day?

**And when he had said these things, all his
adversaries were ashamed: and all the people
rejoiced for all the glorious things that were done
by him.**

LUKE 13:10-17

In this passage, we see the covenant that God has
made with His people. Jesus said in verse 16, **"And ought
not this woman, BEING A DAUGHTER OF
ABRAHAM, whom Satan hath bound, lo, these
eighteen years, be loosed from this bond on the sabbath
day?"** So, you see, this woman was a covenant daughter
of Abraham, and Jesus said she had a right to be free.

In the same way, *we* have a covenant with God, and
we have a right to certain things as a result.

Study closely the following passage.

**Even as Abraham believed God, and it was
accounted to him for righteousness.
Know ye therefore that they which are of faith, the
same are the children of Abraham.
And the scripture, foreseeing that God would
justify the heathen through faith, preached before
the gospel unto Abraham, saying, In thee shall all
nations be blessed.
So then they which be of faith are blessed with
faithful Abraham....**

**Christ hath redeemed us from the curse of the law,
being made a curse for us: for it is written, Cursed
is every one that hangeth on a tree:
That the blessing of Abraham might come on the
Gentiles through Jesus Christ....**

GALATIANS 3:6-9,13,14

Just as it was that woman's right to be loosed from
her infirmity, it is *our* right to be loosed from poverty.
Christ has redeemed us from the curse of the Law. He has
loosed us from the curse of the Law! *Poverty* is a curse just
as *sickness* is a curse. And *prosperity* is a blessing just as
healing is a blessing. Just as we have been legally loosed
from poverty, we can make certain demands on our
covenant and command prosperity — and that includes
money — to come our way. We can *loose* the money for
the need or want!

When we say, "Money, thou art loosed!" we are boldly
testifying and witnessing to the fact that debt,
discontentment, discouragement, and lack cannot hold us
anymore, because we know our covenant rights and we
are using our mouth, not just in words but in power and
in much assurance of faith, to appropriate the money we
need to be on top. And that's where we belong as
children of God — "above only and not beneath" (*see*
Deuteronomy 28:13).

So every time you use the term, "Money, thou art
loosed!" you'll see with the eye of faith money coming to

you because you've taken authority over money. You see, you have to *command* money to come to you. You have to make demands on money. You can't just *wish* it would come; that will never work. You have to use the same authority Jesus used when He said to that woman, "Woman, thou art loosed from thine infirmity!"

Let's look at our passage in Luke 13 again and, in particular, verse 11: **"And, behold, there was a woman which had a spirit of infirmity eighteen years, and was bowed together, and could in no wise lift up herself."** It's easy to gather from this scripture that this woman was bound. Well, did you know that people can be just as bound in their finances? Some are working two and three jobs just to maintain a decent lifestyle and to keep up with all their credit card bills. That's bondage, brother and sister.

Money Bondage Can 'Trip Up' Your Family Life

As I've said many times before, I really believe that God's first intention was that the wife not work. I'm not saying that women who have trained and have worked hard for their careers are supposed to give up their positions. And I'm also not saying that if you're a married woman who's working that you should quit your job tomorrow. That would be foolish. (And don't put pressure on your husband, either, because, as I've also said, prosperity does not come overnight. The world system has both husbands and wives out working, and you can't just get off of that system immediately. You have to get hold of some things first. Then when money starts coming to you and your faith can sustain you, go ahead and make some changes if that's what you want to do.)

I am saying, however, that stress and strain in the area of finances has put more marriages under fire than just about anything else. It can mess up a marriage if you don't know how to handle it. Financial lack can mess up your sex life, because the wife has to come home off the job the same as her husband. Then she has to shift from performing tasks as a breadwinner to performing tasks as wife and perhaps a mother too.

Certainly, I understand that some women have good careers and want to work. I'm not trying to take that from them. But if that's not what you want, you can at least start setting some goals today and begin working toward them. It may take months or even years, but you can get free of both husband and wife having to work just to live decently. And don't be condemned if you're not there yet. Just get ahold of the Word, set some goals, and ask God for wisdom, because you have to start somewhere.

The reason I'm saying all this is, I know the aggravation it can cause when the wife has to go out and help earn a family's living. Many times, husbands get upset when things aren't right in the house, but the reason things aren't right is, she's got two jobs — earning income and taking care of the home and family. I often tell husbands that the reason their dinner may not be cooked properly or be ready on time is, you both pulled up in the driveway from work at the same time. Then the husband usually wants to change clothes and relax, but the wife has to go to her second job, so to speak! (That's why I encourage husbands to help around the house when both partners are working. It would improve their marriage, including their sex life.)

My wife used to work to help earn money for our family, but now she doesn't have to. She works at the ministry, but she doesn't have to. If she wants to take time off to get her hair and nails done, she can do it. She is a wonderful help to me both at the ministry and at home. But the reason is, she's not under pressure about money. That's where God wants us all to be.

Let's continue reading in Luke 13.

> **And, behold, there was a woman which had a spirit of infirmity eighteen years, and was bowed together, and could in no wise lift up herself.**
> **And when Jesus saw her, he called her to him, and said unto her, Woman, thou art loosed from thine infirmity.**
> **And he laid his hands on her: and immediately she was made straight, and glorified God.**
>
> **LUKE 13:11-13**

Notice verse 12. Jesus saw the woman, called her to Himself, and said something to her. What did He say? He said the same thing He is saying to you about debt, poverty, and lack! He said to the woman, "Woman, thou art loosed!" And He is saying to us, "Thou art loosed from debt, poverty, and lack." Therefore, *we* can say, "Money, thou art loosed! Money cometh to me *now*!"

Now notice verse 13: **"And he laid his hands on her: and immediately she was made straight, and glorified God."** You see, your being free glorifies God. And your having a lot of money can glorify Him too. When a child of God puts himself in position for God to bless him, God says, "See My son. He obeyed Me, and I've blessed him. I want the world to see that he's blessed."

It glorifies God when the members of His Church, of His Body, don't need to borrow anything just to get by. It glorifies God when the preacher doesn't have to constantly pump people up to give to the Kingdom. It glorifies Him when people have the money and do what the Lord tells them to do in giving.

And the ruler of the synagogue answered with indignation, because that Jesus had healed on the sabbath day, and said unto the people, There are six days in which men ought to work: in them therefore come and be healed, and not on the sabbath day.

The Lord then answered him, and said, Thou hypocrite, doth not each one of you on the sabbath loose his ox or his ass from the stall, and lead him away to watering?
And ought not this woman, being a daughter of Abraham, whom Satan hath bound, lo, these eighteen years, be loosed from this bond on the sabbath day?

LUKE 13:14-16

Notice verse 16. Jesus said, "Ought not this woman, whom Satan has bound all these years, be loosed from her bond?"

You Ought To Be Loosed!

I want you to read that verse again and think about your debt. If you're married, think about all the arguments you've had with your spouse about money. Think about all the worries and fears you've contended with over money. Those things shouldn't be happening with a child of God, a "daughter of Abraham." You have been given authority over that, and you ought to be loosed!

Jesus was saying that about the woman in Luke 13: "She has no business being bowed over and hump-backed, because she belongs to My company, and I take care of My own!"

Think about that! Jesus was saying, in effect, "My children don't have to go to the world; I'll take care of them. When they claim Me, I claim them. What I have belongs to them. And all the silver and gold, the cattle on a thousand hills, and the earth and the fullness thereof is Mine."

But, while all of this is true, it goes back to this: Whatsoever you loose on earth, He'll loose in Heaven (Matt. 18:18). You see, you have a part to play. So say out loud, "Money, thou art loosed! Money, thou art loosed in my life. Money cometh to me *now!*"

Change Your Thinking — You're in God's Company Now!

When you came into God's company, God took responsibility for you in this earth's realm, because you're making a journey. This earth is not your home; Heaven is. But God has taken responsibility for you right here on the earth, and if you'll remind Him properly, He'll see to it that you have whatever you need or want.

You may have to make a little adjustment if you've been taught that God wants you broke and in poverty. You may have to get some things straight, and it may take your spending more time with God's Word. Did you know that you can live where you want to live, drive what you want to drive, and give what you want to give? You can, but you have to change your thinking first. For example, if you drive by a nice house and say, "I could never see myself living in a house like that," then you never will — not until you make some adjustments in your thinking and in your believing.

When I first started developing in this, I would drive around and look at houses, but I didn't look at small houses. I looked at those big three-story houses. I would walk into some of those houses and my mind would say, *Boo!* But I would say, *You don't scare me. Shut up and don't bother me; I'm looking.*

What was I doing? I was getting an image inside of me of living in a nice big house. I was getting a vision of having a house with nice landscaping and pretty flowers everywhere. So I kept looking. It took me a while — it took years. It took years of my saying to my wife, "Honey, we're going for a drive this evening," and we would ride right out of Poverty Row into neighborhoods where rich folks lived!

'In Due Time'

As I said, we did that for years. And in due time, we had one of those nice big houses! But we did it in *due time*. We wanted a big house, but we wanted it fully furnished too. Then we wanted to be able to have good things for guests to eat when they stopped by. Then if my wife didn't feel like cleaning that big house, I wanted to be able to hire a cleaning company to come in and clean.

All of these things don't take anything but money to have, but you can have the money it takes, because you can say, "Money, thou art loosed!" (But, as I said, you have to do these things in due time and not "ahead of time" or you won't sleep good at night!)

Going back to the woman who was loosed in Luke 13, even though Jesus was talking about this woman's healing in connection with the covenant, we know we can apply what He said to other areas, too, such as finances, because our covenant includes more than healing. We know that He redeemed us from the curse of the Law, which includes sickness, poverty, and spiritual death.

So since Jesus felt so strongly about the covenant of healing being fulfilled in this woman's life, He feels strongly about the covenant of prosperity being fulfilled too. In fact, Jesus feels the same way about every aspect of the covenant, because, as I said, when He redeemed us from the curse of the Law, He redeemed us from sickness, poverty, *and* the Second Death.

God has given us a covenant of prosperity! And because of that covenant, we can believe that God wants us to have more than enough. He wants us to have a full supply, living the abundant life with all our bills paid and money in our pockets and in our bank accounts.

I want you to understand that if you take your place in Christ and do the things God wants you to do concerning money, money has to obey you. It has to be loosed unto you if you command it to be loosed. The

Bible says, **"For if by one man's offence death reigned by one; much more they which receive abundance of grace and of the gift of righteousness shall REIGN IN LIFE by one, Jesus Christ"** (Rom. 5:17).

We are masters of circumstances on this earth, but one area we have not mastered in is money. We need to change our thinking and get so overcome by the Word of God in this area that we can't even *think* broke anymore. We need to get to the place where we can't even *think* about not having enough.

The Revelation of 'Money, Thou Art Loosed!' Is Not Without a Price

Sometimes there is a price to pay when you learn about your authority in Christ and begin to rule and reign over circumstances. For example, people will talk about you. They will persecute you to try to get you to back off the revelation you've received.

Just stay humble and pray for those who persecute you. Jesus said to love your enemies (Matt. 5:44). So keep your attitude straight and continue to go forward in faith doing what you know to do. Go on about your Father's business. Stay in church. Get as many people saved and filled with the Holy Ghost as you can. Others, even family members, may be watching you, waiting for you to fall. But just keep going. With God's Word in your heart, you are not going to fall. (And many of those watching you will end up born again and following the God you serve!)

Some doubt that God wants them to prosper simply because they do not know the Word of God. But God has said, **"Beloved, I wish above all things that thou mayest prosper and be in health, even as thy soul prospereth"** (3 John 2) and **"...I know the thoughts that I think toward you, saith the Lord, thoughts of peace, and not of evil, to give you an expected end"** (Jer. 29:11).

Reading those two verses, along with Luke 13:16, **"...ought not this woman, being a daughter of Abraham, whom Satan hath bound, lo, these eighteen years, be loosed from this bond on the sabbath day?"** I have a question for you. Ought not you prosper and be in health, even as your soul prospers? Ought not you receive your expected end from the Lord since His thoughts are good toward you and not evil? Ought not you be loosed from your bonds of debt, poverty, and lack?

God said in another place, **"...I will dwell in them, and walk in them; and I will be their God, and they shall be my people"** (2 Cor. 6:16). I can just hear the Lord saying, "Ought not those who love Me and who represent Me on the earth be prosperous and walk in health? Ought not they have their needs met over and above just barely getting by — over and above all they can ask or imagine" (Eph. 3:20)? I think you know the answer to that question. *Yes, they ought to!*

'Money, Come Forth!'

Look at John chapter 11 at another important passage that hints at the commanding power we have in Christ.

And when he [Jesus] thus had spoken, he cried with a loud voice, Lazarus, COME FORTH.

JOHN 11:43

Most people are familiar with this account of Lazarus the brother of Martha and Mary who had died and was four days in the grave before Jesus arrived on the scene. But Lazarus' being in that grave four days didn't stop Jesus. He said, "Lazarus, *come forth!*"

Then notice what happened:

And he that was dead came forth, bound hand and foot with graveclothes: and his face was bound about with a napkin. Jesus saith unto them, LOOSE HIM, and let him go.

JOHN 11:44

I tell you, we may have received *some* return on our giving and experienced *some* financial blessings, but we haven't gotten our money loosed yet as we ought. Jesus told Lazarus to come forth. Then He said, "*Loose* him and let him go!"

Notice about Lazarus that he'd been in the grave four days. His sister Martha said to Jesus, "Lord, he stinketh by now" (v. 39). But that didn't stop Jesus. And our "dead," stinky financial condition is not going to stop Him, either! Jesus has already called us to come forth. When He redeemed us by fulfilling God's great plan of redemption, He called us forth out of darkness and into His light. He called us forth out of poverty and into His riches.

But many of us are still bound. We still have on those old graveclothes with that napkin on our face where prosperity is concerned. We haven't seen the truth as we ought, and we have been bound. We haven't been able to walk in the light of prosperity as we ought.

The way we're going to get ourselves untied and get our money untied is by taking hold of the truth by faith and by *commanding* money to be loosed unto us. We can't "try it and see if it works." And we can't wish money were loosed unto us. No, we have to say, *"Money, thou art loosed!"*

From Midnight to Daylight

Now look at Acts 16 where Paul and Silas had been beaten and thrown into prison for preaching the Gospel.

And when they had laid many stripes upon them,
they cast them into prison, charging the jailor to
keep them safely:
Who, having received such a charge, thrust them
into the inner prison, and made their feet fast in
the stocks.
And AT MIDNIGHT Paul and Silas prayed, and
sang praises unto God: and the prisoners heard
them.
And suddenly there was a great earthquake, so that
the foundations of the prison were shaken: and
immediately all the doors were opened, and every
one's bands were LOOSED.

ACTS 16:23-26

Some people have been experiencing "midnight" in
their finances, but Jesus and the Word have come to bring
them daylight.

Do you know what I mean by "midnight"? I mean,
it's dark in the arena of your finances. You love God. You
attend church and respect your pastor. You serve God and
walk in love toward others. But it's dark in your finances.
You need an opening somewhere for light to come in on
your situation.

Well, this passage tells you how to do it. It says, "...at
**midnight Paul and Silas PRAYED, and SANG PRAISES
unto God: and the prisoners heard them."**

Something ought to happen when you pray and sing praises. Something ought to happen in your finances if you've been in the dark — if it's been midnight in your finances. When you pray in faith and sing praises to God because you believe it's done and the answer is on its way, you shouldn't continue to be broke and in the dark financially.

What happened when Paul and Silas prayed and sang praises to God? Verse 26 says, **"And suddenly there was a great earthquake, so that the foundations of the prison were shaken: and immediately all the doors were opened, and EVERY ONE'S BANDS WERE LOOSED"**!

'Suddenly' and 'Immediately'

That's what can happen for you, too, when you pray and sing praises to God. Notice something else about that verse. It says, **". . . SUDDENLY there was a great earthquake. . . and IMMEDIATELY all the doors were opened, and every one's bands were loosed."** God knows how to turn things around for you *suddenly* and cause things to *immediately* become better for you!

Let's read that entire verse. **"And suddenly there was a great earthquake, so that the foundations of the prison were shaken: and immediately all the doors were opened, and every one's bands were loosed."** Talking about your finances, you could read that verse this way: "Suddenly, there was a great earthquake, so that the foundations of *debt, distress, discontentment, lack,* and *poverty* were shaken: and immediately all the doors were opened, and everyone's bands were loosed."

The Lord once told me, "I'm going to do a quick work. I'm going to show signs and wonders in the area of finances, because My people have been behind too long. Those who take Me at My Word, I'm going to do a quick work in their finances."

God wants to shake the foundation of your money problem and open doors of opportunity for you to have plenty!

Signs and Wonders in Your Finances

Some people think they're scripturally inclined, but they can't even hear God. They have their own ideas about certain things — in particular, about money — and they won't hear anything else. I'm going to put a hole in your boat, so to speak, if you are one of those people who believe that God doesn't want you to have plenty of money. The Lord once told me, "I desire to do signs and wonders in and with the finances of every one of My children, because they've been so far behind. The only way I can really bring them up in their finances before Jesus comes is to do miracles in their finances."

Many people have thought that signs and wonders are only about lame people walking again, blind people receiving their sight, deaf people receiving their hearing, and the dead being raised. But God wants to perform signs and wonders in people's *finances* too.

However, first, God wants you to have an awareness of the vastness of His abilities in the area of finances in your life. He wants you to possess an awareness of the great bridge He has built over poverty. He wants you to know the quality and the reality of His Word. The power to create miracles — signs and wonders — in your finances will not be activated until you learn to depend totally on the Word. Your faith has to be unhindered by religious beliefs and traditions of the past that you have perhaps been holding on to.

Money's Purpose

Why does God want us to have plenty of money? There is a reason. Money has a purpose in the mind of God: *to get the lost saved; to demonstrate that the devil's works have been destroyed;* and *to cause people to experience life more abundantly* (John 10:10) in the area of finances.

The following passage illustrates the *first* purpose for money: *to get the lost saved.*

> **And Jesus entered and passed through Jericho.**
> **And, behold, there was a man named Zacchaeus, which was the chief among the publicans, and he was rich.**
> **And he sought to see Jesus who he was; and could not for the press, because he was little of stature.**
> **And he ran before, and climbed up into a sycomore tree to see him: for he was to pass that way.**
> **And when Jesus came to the place, he looked up, and saw him, and said unto him, Zacchaeus, make haste, and come down; for to day I must abide at thy house.**
> **And he made haste, and came down, and received him joyfully.**

And when they saw it, they all murmured, saying,
That he was gone to be guest with a man that is a
sinner.
And Zacchaeus stood, and said unto the Lord;
Behold, Lord, the half of my goods I give to the
poor; and if I have taken any thing from any man
by false accusation, I restore him fourfold.
And Jesus said unto him, This day is salvation
come to this house forsomuch as he also is a son of
Abraham.
For the Son of man is come to seek and to save that
which was lost.

LUKE 19:1-10

Look at verse 10: **"For the Son of man is come to seek
and to save that which was lost."** *The saving of the lost is
the first purpose for money.* In order to prosper as God
wants you to, you have to get that straight in your heart.
You have to be committed to being a prime supporter of
saving the lost, and that takes money. You have to have
the attitude, *God, give money to me, and I'll give it up as You
tell me to — as You lead and guide me. I will not only be*
obedient *to give it, but* willing *to give it.*

So your first purpose for having money is to finance
the spreading of the Gospel and to give as God speaks to
you. Many Christians aren't able to give money when the
preacher makes some special plea. In other words, the
man of God might say, "We need to send these

missionaries to such-and-such place." But many are not stable enough financially to give very much. Some of those people come from traditional, denominational backgrounds where they were taught that poverty was a mark of godliness. They were told, "Stay away from that money because money will carry you into pride."

Listen, brother and sister, if your heart is right with God, money is not going to take you into pride. If anything, it will humble you more, because you know where it came from. You know it didn't come from you. You know that when you went from poverty to riches that it was God who brought you out and got you to the place of prosperity and of having plenty of money.

We've been deceived about money. Even those who have been tithing have not largely been receiving back from their tithe as they should, because of deception and a lack of knowledge. Many haven't released their tithe with joy. They just put their tithe in the offering bucket dutifully, but that's not the way to receive the blessing of the tithe. You have to release *faith* to receive the blessing of the tithe.

Let's look at Zacchaeus again. You remember when Jesus saw Zacchaeus in that tree, Jesus said to him, **"... make haste, and come down; for to day I must abide at thy house"** (Luke 19:5). Zacchaeus "received Him joyfully" (v. 6) and said, **"... Behold, Lord, the half of my goods I give to the poor; and if I have taken any thing from any man by false**

accusation, I restore him fourfold" (v. 8). Zacchaeus gave up His money to the Lord joyfully; he had the right attitude toward Jesus.

I'm talking about purpose and having a right attitude toward God about money. God wants His job done on the earth, but when you give to His work, He has you covered too. In other words, He has your needs and wants — the "extra" — covered. As I've said many times before, there's nothing you can't have if you hook up properly with God — if you give your all to Him spirit, soul, and body.

Many people pay their tithes, but, beyond the tithe, which is something we *owe*, they haven't taken authority over their giving. They won't tell the Lord He can have it all if He wants it.

God doesn't usually tell people to give all their money away, but I believe He wants to hear you say from your heart that you'd give it up to Him. Why? For *purpose* — for the purpose of getting the lost saved. Jesus said, **"For the Son of man is come to seek and to save that which was lost"** (Luke 19:10). Your money has something to do with that. Your money has something to do with the end-time harvest of souls. Your money has something to do with the operation of the local church. When you fully realize that, then when God tells you to give, you will know that He is working something out. He is getting His work done, and He is getting you in position to receive even more. He will speak to others on your behalf. He will cause you to find favor.

Let's look at another verse of Scripture dealing with purpose.

8 ...For this PURPOSE the Son of God was manifested, that he might destroy the works of the devil.

1 JOHN 3:8

The *second* purpose for having money — for walking in divine prosperity — is *to demonstrate that the devil's works of poverty have been destroyed in your life.*

Certainly we know that Christ has redeemed us from the curse of the Law (Gal. 3:13), and one of the curses for breaking God's Law is poverty. God has made a covenant of prosperity with us through Christ. So we know that Christ has redeemed us from poverty in His death, burial, and resurrection. Satan and his works, including poverty, are destroyed in our lives; he is a defeated foe. But we have to *enforce* Satan's defeat by faith in the Word of God. We have to *appropriate* that which legally belongs to us and demonstrate that the devil's works are destroyed in our lives.

But, as I said, walking in your inheritance in Christ is not an overnight process. You walk in your inheritance by degrees, according to your faith. That's why many give up on prosperity — because it doesn't happen for them fast enough. Then they get offended and say, "That prosperity stuff doesn't work."

But if we want increase and signs and wonders in our finances, we need to be honest with ourselves and with God. We need to judge Him faithful, because He is faithful that promised, and He is not a man that He should lie (Heb. 10:23; Num. 23:19).

Hindrances to Financial Increase

Did you know that becoming impatient, offended, or full of strife will hinder your progress in walking in prosperity and receiving signs and wonders in your finances? For example, I know of men who don't bring enough income into their household, yet they expect their wife to pay all the bills and make ends meet somehow. Then when she can't, they get mad and want to know what happened!

I'll tell you what happened in more cases than one — those men were not using their faith! They just left their wife with the responsibility of trying to pay everyone they owe and of believing God to make it all work. Not only did those men become impatient and offended, some of them were too lazy spiritually to believe God for themselves!

Do you want to know another reason why you need money? A lot of marriage relationships aren't working right and a lot of love is being missed over this little thing called poverty. Many marriages end in divorce over money. Money has something to do with every avenue of our lives. So having money not only demonstrates that the devil's works of poverty are destroyed in our lives, but that his works of strife, broken relationships, and divorce are destroyed too!

Someone might say, "Well, I just don't believe First John 3:8 has anything to do with money." But it *does* have something to do with money. For example, we need to have money to keep the church operating properly so we can get the Gospel out and get young people off drugs. Can you agree that illicit drugs are a work of the devil?

Ask yourself these questions: "How are the devil's works going to be destroyed if Christians don't have any money?" "How are his works going to be destroyed if the church is broke?" "How are we going to attract sinners if we are broke and in debt?"

Prosperity Is a Mark of the Covenant

One of the marks of the covenant that God set up with man is wealth. Abraham, Isaac, and Jacob, for example, were wealthy. People recognized that those men had a certain standing with God. And do you remember how God bragged on Job?

There was a man in the land of Uz, whose name
was Job; and that man was perfect and upright, and
one that feared God, and eschewed evil.
And there were born unto him seven sons and
three daughters.
His substance also was seven thousand sheep, and
three thousand camels, and five hundred yoke of
oxen, and five hundred she asses, and a very great
household; so that this man was the greatest of all
the men of the east.

JOB 1:1-3

When God bragged on Job, one of the things He
talked about was Job's substance. Why? Because Job was
upright before God and feared Him and shunned evil.
And I believe that what Job had was a result of his walk
with God.

God will increase you no matter where you're at. If
you're broke and in debt, God will increase you and
enable you to be debt-free. If you're already enjoying a
certain degree of God's financial blessings, He will see to
it that you get more. So wherever you are, this message is
for you. God wants to do signs and wonders in your
finances.

God Wants You To Enjoy Life

The *third* purpose for your having money is closely
related to the second one, but you can't enter into the

third one until you've accomplished the second — until you are demonstrating that the devil's works of poverty and lack have been and are being destroyed in your life. (As a matter of fact, you can't go on to the third purpose until you obey the *first* purpose of using your finances to help spread the Gospel.)

What is the third purpose? *To cause people to experience life more abundantly* (John 10:10) in the area of finances!

> **The thief cometh not, but for to steal, and to kill, and to destroy: I am come that they might have life, and that they might have it more abundantly.**
> **JOHN 10:10**

Not only does God want you out of debt, but He wants you to have abundance. He not only wants you to have your *needs* met, He wants you to have your *desires* met too.

Look at that word "more" in the phrase "more abundantly." As I said, no matter where you're at, God wants you to have more. Some people measure their prosperity by other people's lack. But that's not prosperity — both sides could be broke! God wants everyone to move up in this at his own pace.

God's original plan was for us never to experience poverty. But you remember Adam sold out to the devil, and the devil became the god of this world (2 Cor. 4:4). Now if you are a Christian, God is your God, and He is more powerful than the devil, the god of this world. But in order for you to experience life more abundantly, you must cooperate with Him.

You see, you are God's contact on the earth. You are His channel whereby He can do supernatural things in people's lives. He can't just do things on the earth without your faith and cooperation.

God Wants To Put You 'Over'

Let's look more closely at how God originally set this thing up. God's first plan for His man, Adam, was that he be a wealthy man. God placed him over everything in that Garden.

> **And God said, Let us make man in our image, after our likeness: and let them have dominion OVER the fish of the sea, and OVER the fowl of the air, and OVER the cattle, and OVER all the earth, and OVER every creeping thing that creepeth upon the earth.**
>
> **GENESIS 1:26**

God set Adam up to have dominion. Notice the word "over" in this verse. God gave Adam dominion *over* fish, fowl, cattle, and over all the earth. Money, or silver and gold, is included in that statement!

We know that Adam lost or gave up his dominion when he disobeyed God and sold out to Satan. But the Second Adam, Jesus Christ (1 Cor. 15:22,45), came that we might take back our dominion over certain things — over Satan and circumstances. As believers today, we are supposed to have dominion over money. Yet money has been dominating us by our not having enough.

Remember we read that the silver and the gold are the Lord's (Haggai 2:8). Well, where is the gold and silver that are the Lord's? It's in the earth. But because Satan is the god of this world, God can't just sovereignly give us the "over" and the "dominion" that we read about in Genesis 1:26. No, He has to have our cooperation. If we'll learn to cooperate with Him, He'll put us right back in the Garden of Eden, so to speak, where we can have more than enough of everything we need!

God is a great supplier. All we have to do is continue reading in Genesis to see what a great supplier God is.

And God BLESSED them, and God said unto them, Be fruitful, and multiply, and replenish the earth, and subdue it: and have dominion over the fish of the sea, and over the fowl of the air, and over every living thing that moveth upon the earth.

GENESIS 1:28

And the Lord God planted a garden eastward in
Eden; and there he put the man whom he had
formed.
And out of the ground made the Lord God to grow
every tree that is pleasant to the sight, and good for
food; the tree of life also in the midst of the garden,
and the tree of knowledge of good and evil.
And a river went out of Eden to water the garden;
and from thence it was parted, and became into
four heads.
The name of the first is Pison: that is it which
compasseth the whole land of Havilah, where there
is gold;
And the gold of that land is good: there is bdellium
and the onyx stone.

GENESIS 2:8-12

If what God did for His man, Adam, was not
prosperity, then tell me what prosperity is! These verses
ought to do away with every notion that money is evil. I
tell you, it's more evil *not* to have it, because having it is
God's plan and purpose for us.

Now look at verse 12 where it talks about gold,
bdellium, and onyx. We know what gold is, but what is
this bdellium? It was a white pearl, a valuable mineral of
Havilah. So there was gold and pearl in the Garden of
Eden. And the onyx, which was there also, was a precious

stone that the high priest of the Old Testament wore on his garment.

Don't Be Ignorant of Satan's Devices To Trick You Out of Your Prosperity

I tell you, Adam was not broke! But do you know what happened? Satan came along and tricked him out of his prosperity, just as Satan tries to trick *us* out of *our* prosperity today. How does he do it? He does it a number of ways — through leading us to believe that it is godly to be broke, through false teaching about the faith message, and through unforgiveness and other sin.

If you think it is godly to be broke and that it's evil to have money, you are not going to trust God to help you get any, are you? And if you don't know how to walk by faith, you are not going to be able to appropriate the divine provision of prosperity. And if your heart is not right because you have something against someone in your heart, what faith you have developed will be hindered. Do you see how Satan tries to trick people out of their prosperity?

You can't afford to hold a grudge against someone. When someone wrongs you, you have to let it go so you can keep yourself in position for God to pour His blessings out on you. Unforgiveness will short-circuit the power of God in your life and will keep you from seeing the signs and wonders in your finances that you want to see. But you can let unforgiveness go. I'm telling you that you can because God says you can. He says, **"... Vengeance is mine; I will repay, saith the Lord"** (Rom. 12:19).

Dare To Step Out and Walk Free of Poverty and Lack

Do you want to break loose in your finances? Do you want to see signs and wonders in your finances? If so, I *dare* you to appropriate prosperity by faith according to God's Word. I *dare* you to turn loose of your tithe if you haven't been tithing. I *dare* you to increase your giving of offerings. God will show Himself strong on your behalf if you will cooperate with Him and get in line with His purpose for prosperity.

I'm not talking about something I haven't experienced personally. I have some extremely wealthy businessmen in my church, but I once told the Lord, "I want to be the biggest giver in my church." I opened my heart up to Him, and, today, I am the biggest giver in my church!

Listen, friend, when you give to God and He gives back to you, He dumps prosperity on you like a dump truck! But if you are tight and stingy, He won't be able to give you much, because He can't trust you. He knows that if He gives you something, you're going to hoard it up for yourself and forget Him and His work.

God Gives Increase to the Faithful

I'm teaching you how to come into the Master's plan. Some people can't open their heart up to God to say to Him, "Lord, I want to be the biggest giver in my church," because they aren't even giving what they have now. They are holding on tight to the little they have when they ought to be releasing it. That little they have can't compare to what God wants them to have. But He can't give it to them because they aren't cooperating with Him. He said, **"He that is faithful in that which is least is faithful also in much: and he that is unjust in the least is unjust also in much"** (Luke 16:10).

You remember in the parable of the talents, the master took the one talent from the man who'd taken his one talent and hidden it. He didn't do anything with the little God had given him. Then the master gave it to the man who'd doubled his talents (*see* Matthew 25:14-30). As a young Gospel boy, I used to read that and think, *Man! What was God doing?* But I found out that's the way God deals. He increases the one who is faithful.

When money becomes your god — you're holding on to it tight and being unfaithful in your giving — then God can't increase you supernaturally. He wants to, but He can't, because you are trusting in your money and not in Him.

In a previous chapter, I touched on this briefly in connection with Deuteronomy 8:18, "... **it is he** [God]

that giveth thee power to get wealth.... " I said that God doesn't actually give us money or wealth; He gives us the *power* to get wealth.

Let me show you why God can't actually give you money.

> **In whom the GOD OF THIS WORLD** [Satan] **hath blinded the minds of them which believe not, lest the light of the glorious gospel of Christ, who is the image of God, should shine unto them.**
> **2 CORINTHIANS 4:4**

As I said before, Satan is the god of this world. He became the god of this world when Adam sold out to him in the Garden of Eden. Satan is the god of this world system. That's why God can't give you wealth. He doesn't have currency in Heaven that He can just rain down on you. Certainly, He can use people to get money to you, but He doesn't rain money down from Heaven, because then He would be a counterfeiter. And we know that God is not a counterfeiter.

No, God has to give you the power to get the wealth that is already in the world. And that wealth — all the silver and gold, the cattle on a thousand hills, and the earth and the fullness thereof — legally belongs to God (Haggai 2:8; Ps. 50:10; 89:11). But to get it, you are going to have to have power. You are going to have to claim what rightfully belongs to you, and you are going to have to understand how to *cooperate* with God's power (we already talked about faith and obedience — tithing and giving offerings — as ways to cooperate with God).

Supernatural Increase Is God's Will for You!

Just because God can't rain money down on you from Heaven doesn't mean that He doesn't want you to have it. He does want you to have money. And if you already have some money, God wants you to have more. Increase is God's will for you.

Why? Because when you increase financially, His vision on earth increases. When you increase, it is a sign of the goodness and the fatherhood of God toward His children that the whole world can see. Matthew 7:11 says, **"If ye then, being evil** [or natural], **know how to give good gifts unto your children, how much more shall your Father which is in heaven give good things to them that ask him?"**

More and More

How much more power to get wealth will God give you? *More and more. More* than enough. *More* than you need. *More* than you give. *More* than you can ask or think. That's the kind of God we serve!

I tell you, God has a full supply waiting on you to tap into by acting on His Word. There are so many scriptures in the Word that hold the key to tapping into this supply. For example, Psalm 23:1 says, **"The Lord is my shepherd; I SHALL not want."**

Then there are other verses that promise prosperity and use that little word "shall."

> **Give, and it SHALL be given unto you; good measure, pressed down, and shaken together, and running over, shall men give into your bosom. For with the same measure that ye mete withal it shall be measured to you again.**
>
> **LUKE 6:38**

Now I know those verses talk about more than just financial prosperity, but financial prosperity is included.

Let's look at one more.

> **But my God SHALL supply all your need according to his riches in glory by Christ Jesus.**
>
> **PHILIPPIANS 4:19**

That word "shall" is one of the strongest words in the English language. There is no mistaking the meaning of that word. When it says, "The Lord is my shepherd; I shall not want." it means I *shall* not want! Yet many have been saying that they're *full* of want. They've heard their parents saying it, their grandparents saying it, and their great-grandparents saying it! But when God uses the word "shall" in a statement, it is a sure thing if we'll take hold of it.

By now I hope you understand that it is God's will that you prosper and increase in your finances. God is a good God, but He can't demonstrate His goodness to you just because He's good. He has to have some faith and some cooperation on your part in order to get more money into your hands.

God Will Do a Quick Work

Just how is God going to get more money to you? As I said before, He's going to give you the power to get wealth. But just how is He going to do it? The Lord once said to me, "In order to get the money back in the hands of My children, I'm going to release signs and wonders in their finances. Miracles, signs, and wonders are the only means for them to catch up to where I always wanted them to be."

In other words, we don't have enough time left for us to go the old confession route. Certainly, we have to maintain our faith and our confession. But the way I understand it is, God is going to add a *booster* to our confession so that we can experience miracles, signs, and wonders in our finances. He said, "I will do a *quick* work with their money so that they will know that it is of Me."

However, we are going to have to be convinced of God's will to prosper us and then we are going to have to be bold about it. We are going to have to believe, tithe, give, stand on God's sure Word, and tell Satan to take his hands off our money! We are going to have to tell him to "Loose it and let it go!" and then constantly make the confession, "My money is loosed in Jesus' Name."

If you think of the speed of a jet plane flying overhead, that is how fast things are going to happen in many people's finances. And if you think of the number of stars in the sky on a clear night, that is how much money He's going to pour on the members of the Body of Christ who take hold of this revelation.

The Place of Honor in Receiving Financial Signs and Wonders

That all sounds wonderful, and I'm telling it to you the way the Lord told it to me. But here is the sobering part. The Lord also said to me, "How can I esteem one who does not esteem Me? How can I honor someone who does not honor Me?"

Now I'm not saying that to talk you out of faith or to talk you out of your miracle. Just make a little adjustment on the inside if you have not been esteeming God's Word or honoring Him with your income — with tithes and offerings. You know the adjustment you personally need to make without anyone telling you what to do. God only wants to bless us, so I believe it would behoove all of us to make our adjustment right now!

When you give more, more will come to you. That is a spiritual principle that we see over and over again in the Word. For example, the Word says, **"...He which soweth sparingly shall reap also sparingly; and he which soweth bountifully shall reap also bountifully"** (2 Cor. 9:6). You can't be ready for a harvest without having sown first. And you can't be ready for a big harvest without have sown big first!

I'm talking about signs and wonders in your finances. Someone said, "Yes, Reverend Thompson, but can you give me an example of a sign and a wonder in the Bible concerning money?" Well, anytime a fish comes up with money in its mouth, that's a sign and a wonder! And Peter didn't have to pick up a bunch of fish to find that money. It was in the first fish he picked up!

**And when they were come to Capernaum, they that received tribute money came to Peter, and said, Doth not your master pay tribute?
He saith, Yes. And when he was come into the house, Jesus prevented him, saying, What thinkest thou, Simon? of whom do the kings of the earth take custom or tribute? of their own children, or of strangers?
Peter saith unto him, Of strangers. Jesus saith unto him, Then are the children free.
Notwithstanding, lest we should offend them, go thou to the sea, and cast an hook, and take up the**

**fish that first cometh up; and when thou hast
opened his mouth, thou shalt find a piece of
money: that take, and give unto them for me and
thee.**

MATTHEW 17:24-27

That is what I call taking authority over money! Jesus
talked to the waves and the wind, and they obeyed Him.
He talked to bread, and it multiplied. Jesus talked to
someone who was in the grave four days, and the man
got up and came out of that grave! And Jesus talked to a
fish, and that fish brought Peter some money!

I tell you, there is only one Jesus — one Messiah, one
Anointed One. There has never been, nor will there ever
be, anyone who walked like Him or talked like Him.
There's only one, so don't fall for some of the junk you
hear on television. It's foolishness to believe that there is
another Messiah. There is only one, and His Name is
Jesus. He's sitting at the right hand of the Father, and
He's my Intercessor, my Mediator, my High Tower. And
I'll tell you something else. This Jesus is the Lord of
prosperity and the Lord over poverty!

I wonder about these religious cult leaders who
would try to lead you to believe they are the Messiah. Did
they ever rise up from the dead on the third day? Did
they ever use a cloud as an elevator in which to ascend
up into Heaven? Did they ever reverse the tug of gravity?
No, they never did. Can they really make old things pass

away and make all things become new? Can they give you rest when you are laden with burdens? Can they give you peace in place of your anxiety? Can they hear your cry among a million voices and bring you out of your test or trial? Can they deliver you from sin, set your feet on solid ground, and guarantee you a place in Heaven? No, they can't — they are false prophets.

Jesus is the King of kings and Lord of lords, and He wants to be your Lord in every area of your life, including your finances. Money is not the primary thing. The key to walking with the Lord is to live right and in fellowship with Him, and as He moves you in new directions by His Spirit, just go on and move with Him.

This can be a turning point in your life, friend. As you honor and delight yourself in the Word of God and His Presence, things you couldn't see before, you're going to start seeing. God will manifest His glory in your life as He never has before. And it's going to affect your financial situation. You will never be the same again. God will give you such power to get wealth that you'll be a premiere supporter of the Gospel.

I heard the Lord say about those who will obey Him, "I'll anoint you for prosperity as you've never seen before. You will be one of the ones who will carry the load of spreading My Word in these last days. But the load will not be so heavy, because I'll be carrying you."

I also heard the Lord say, "Walk in love with your brothers and sisters. Walk in love. Walk in faith. Walk in sowing and reaping, and walk in the spirit of life in Christ Jesus. You'll see things happen in your life that you thought couldn't happen. Promotion will come. You will be promoted in My Kingdom, in My anointing, in My blessing, and in your finances, and you'll be blessed as you've never been blessed before. So yield to My Spirit and to the things I have spoken to you, and it will not be hard, but it will be easy."

One scripture I've mentioned several times is Jeremiah 29:11, which says, **"For I know the thoughts that I think toward you, saith the Lord, thoughts of peace, and not of evil, to give you an expected end."** Let's read that in the *New International Version*: "'For I know the plans I have for you,' declares the Lord, 'plans to prosper you and not to harm you, plans to give you hope and a future.'"

God wants to give you hope and a future where money is concerned. The devil has been stealing, killing, and destroying in the area of finances. He wants to make the church world look bad and the world look good. Jesus said, **"...I am come that they might have life, and that they might have it more abundantly"** (John 10:10). But we know that the Body of Christ is not living in the abundance that has been provided for them because they've been robbed through religion and the doctrines of men.

But you don't have to be robbed. Money can be loosed unto you; you can make money obey you. Money doesn't have to be resistant to you. Getting money loosed unto you can be the easiest thing. But you can't just mess around with the Word of the God and the revelation He gives you. You can't just have the attitude, *I'm satisfied till*

I get to Heaven or *The church will make it without my tithes and offerings as long as folks keep coming to our pot-luck dinners.* That's what religion has taught us, but it's not the Word of God.

No, you have to be bold with your spiritual authority. And that authority is not just for money, either. When you get things lined up with God and His Word, healing will have to obey you; long life and peace will have to obey you; and money will have to obey you. Money will have to turn toward you when you make your declaration in faith, "Money, thou art loosed in my life!"

Knowing and walking in your authority makes you dangerous to the kingdom of darkness. You see, knowing your rights in Christ and what belongs to you in Him is not just for you; it's for the world. You can't help someone else if you are powerless. You can't get someone saved if you don't have a revelation of what God did in Christ for the whole world. The work has been finished. Now we have to be bold about proclaiming it.

Now what am I saying when I say, "Money, thou art loosed in my life"? I'm saying, "Satan, you have to turn my money loose. I know my authority. I am not an ignorant Christian. And you have to turn mine loose!"

Did you know that there is plenty of money in the earth right now — enough to make every believer rich? God originally deposited enough prosperity in the earth for every one of His children to have more than enough. If that's not true, then He lied about it when He told us that the Lord is our Shepherd; we shall not want. Or He lied about it when He said He was El Shaddai, the God who is more than enough. Or He lied about it when He said He would supply all of our need.

But God didn't lie. He has made provision whereby we can always have all-sufficiency (2 Cor. 9:8). Now it's up to us to take hold of that. If we're broke, it's not God's fault for the condition we're in. We've settled for it. We haven't known any better. But we can make a little adjustment today. We can get things turned around and changed in our lives.

If your covenant with God, which includes prosperity, is powerful enough to loose the woman with the issue of blood, to bring Lazarus back from the dead and get him out of his grave clothes, and to cause an earthquake to shake the doors of the prison loose for Paul and Silas, then that covenant is powerful enough to cause an "earthquake" in your financial situation, loosing money to you so that you can have abundance!

When you came into the Kingdom, you came into prosperity. God just wants you to follow orders, that's all.

"What do you mean, 'Follow orders'?" I mean, follow His Word and follow His prompting when He wants you to do something. Sell out to Him, and that includes selling out in the area of finances. Remember I said that you can't take authority over your receiving until you've taken authority over your giving. In other words, you can't say, "Money, thou art loosed" if you're not giving in accordance with God's Word. What does that mean — "in accordance with God's Word"? That means giving willingly and cheerfully from your heart. It means giving in faith and trust. It means sowing bountifully so that you may reap a bountiful harvest. It means looking to Him instead of trying to accumulate wealth in your own power or strength.

God is saying to us, "Come to Me and My Word. Come up higher in your finances. Stop trying to handle things yourself."

God Sees Your Condition

If you've ever tried to take care of things in your own strength, you know it doesn't work! Have you ever tried to take care of something in your own power? You didn't get very far, did you? And all the while, God was watching. He saw your condition and wanted to help.

Let me show you something about the woman with the issue of blood. Look at Luke 13:11 and 12.

And, behold, there was a woman which had a spirit of infirmity eighteen years, and was bowed together, and could in no wise lift up herself. AND WHEN JESUS SAW HER, he called her to him, and said unto her, Woman, thou art loosed from thine infirmity.

LUKE 13:11,12

Notice verse 12: **"And when Jesus SAW her...."** Jesus saw the condition this woman was in, and He sees our condition too. We know from reading this passage that when Jesus saw the condition of this woman, He did something. What did He do? He said to her, **"...Woman, thou art loosed from thine infirmity."**

Jesus is saying to us today, "Thou art loosed from thine condition." He's already paid the price. We don't have to sit around, hoping He'll come to our house and tell us we're loosed. No, He's already loosed us, and now we have to agree with Him and proclaim that we are loosed!

Jesus sees the condition of the Body of Christ. Financially, many are in distress, in debt, and in discontentment. Financial lack is a terrible thing. As I said before, a lot of divorce happens because of finances. A lot of fights between husbands and wives happen because of finances. A lot of sleepless nights and worry and frustration happen because of money.

But Jesus sees our condition, and we can rest assured that He's already done something about it. And we can experience what He's done for us if we'll rise up and take our place in faith and walk in the authority that He has given us.

Part of Knowing Your Authority
Is Knowing Your Rights

Looking back at the woman with the issue of blood, when Jesus saw her condition, He didn't like it. That woman was a daughter of Abraham; she was living under the Abrahamic covenant, which included healing. Jesus hadn't even gone to the Cross yet to die in our place and fulfill the New Covenant, but this woman still had a covenant right.

How much more do we have a covenant right to be free today! More so, because we are on the other side of Calvary. Jesus is in Heaven, seated at the right hand of God as our Mediator and High Priest. He doesn't like seeing us in some condition that He died for. He doesn't like seeing us trying to deal with things He's already paid the price for.

Jesus told His followers after He had risen from the dead that He had all authority and that He was assigning that authority to them.

> **And Jesus came and spake unto them, saying, ALL POWER** [authority] **is given unto me in heaven and in earth.**
> **Go ye therefore, and teach all nations, baptizing them in the name of the Father, and of the Son, and of the Holy Ghost:**

Teaching them to observe all things whatsoever I have commanded you: and, lo, I am with you alway, even unto the end of the world. Amen.
MATTHEW 28:18-20

Jesus has given us all this authority, but it is largely going to waste. You also remember we read Matthew 18:18, in which Jesus says, **"Verily I say unto you, Whatsoever ye shall bind on earth shall be bound in heaven: and whatsoever ye shall loose on earth shall be loosed in heaven."**

I can just imagine Jesus saying, "Do you believe Me? Do you believe what I said about your authority? Do you believe that whatsoever you loose on earth, I'll loose in Heaven? Don't you know that when I loose something, it's loosed? And don't you know that no one can tie up something that I've loosed?"

There's no lock strong enough to lock what Jesus has loosed! There's no rope or chain strong enough to hold back what He's loosed. I tell you, the devil does not have a big enough rope to hold you back and keep you broke!

Someone asked, "If all this is true, why aren't more people loosing their money, telling Satan to take his hands off their finances?" I think it's a lack of knowledge of the Word of God — of God's will for them concerning finances and of their spiritual authority. One thing that's holding them back is their belief in the false notion that money is evil. "I don't want to talk about money," they'll say. "I love the Lord."

You see, the devil doesn't mind if people shout and get happy in church on Sunday. Do you know why? Because he doesn't mind your shouting on Sunday when he knows he's got you on Monday and on every other day of the week, because you're shouting without knowledge.

Some people get all excited at the moment a certain message is preached or when God is moving in a certain way. But the excitement wears off because they don't know what to do down the road when depression or circumstances try to hit them. Then others "fake it" when they're shouting. They're dead and dry on the inside, because the Word is not in them. But you don't have to fake it. It is a fact that whatsoever you loose on earth, the Lord said, "I'll loose it in Heaven." So get that truth on the inside of you, and you won't have to fake it anymore.

Now when the Lord said, "I'll loose it in Heaven," He's not talking about loosing something in Heaven. Yes, Jesus is in Heaven, but He is "loosing" *from* Heaven, not *in* Heaven. In Heaven, your blessings won't need to be loosed, because they are not bound up! No, Jesus was talking about loosing something on the earth.

As I said before, the money you need is already in the earth. Some people think that when you loose money on the earth, the Lord looses money in Heaven. But, no, the Lord in Heaven looses money on the earth. The Lord is saying, "When you loose money, using your authority on the earth, I will loose the ability to cause that which you said to come to pass."

Let me tell you something else about this scripture, **"...Whatsoever ye shall bind on earth shall be bound in heaven: and whatsoever ye shall loose on earth shall be loosed in heaven"** (Matt. 18:18). It's as if the Lord is also saying, "Whatsoever you *don't* bind on the earth shall *not* be bound in Heaven. And whatsoever you *don't* loose on earth shall *not* be loosed in Heaven." In other words, He's saying, "I can't permit it unless you permit it." So we know that if *we* permit money to come to us — if we loose it — *God* will permit it to come to us. He will loose it. And when God looses something, friend, it is loosed!

God Is a Right- Now God!

For example, in Luke 13, in the case of the woman who was bowed down and could in no wise lift up herself, it says, **"...when Jesus saw her, he called her to him, and said unto her, Woman, thou art loosed from thine infirmity"** (v. 12). When Jesus said, "Woman, thou art loosed," how long do you think it took for her to be loosed?

And he laid his hands on her: and IMMEDIATELY she was made straight, and glorified God.

LUKE 13:13

How quickly did she receive her deliverance? It says she *immediately* was made straight. Here's what the Spirit of God said unto me, "I desire to do signs and wonders in the finances of the Body of Christ. In order to get the money back into the hands of My children, I'm going to release signs and wonders in their finances." In other words, God is going to do some things "immediately" and "suddenly" in people's lives!

Not everyone is going to experience the miraculous in his or her finances because not everyone will believe. But those who believe and act upon the message they've heard will come out of debt, distress, and discontentment and will glorify God. They will have more than enough, and they will finance the spreading of the Gospel and help usher in Christ's return.

God Takes Responsibility for His Children

Some Christians have a problem believing that their prosperity glorifies God. But let me ask you something. Since the Bible says, for example, **"The Lord is my shepherd; I shall not want"** (Ps. 23:1), does it glorify God when you're not in want or when you are in want, lack, poverty and distress? It doesn't glorify God when His children go around as if they're orphans or they're fatherless. No, God's children have a good "Daddy." He provides for His own. He doesn't need welfare or any help from the government to take care of His children. All He needs is His child's submission to Him. He needs his faith and obedience.

God is your Father if you are born again. You can say to Him, "You are my Daddy. You are responsible for me, and I am responsible to obey You." God is not a deserting Father. He is not an absentee Father. He didn't leave you in the hands of pastors, teachers, prophets, and evangelists. Certainly, He gave us those ministry gifts for a reason, but He takes personal responsibility for us.

And Christ did not leave the Bride without a Husband. The Husband takes care of His family. We've been wrestling with this world system, trying to get some financial support. Forget those long lines and all that paperwork! Just have a talk with your Daddy. Have a talk with your Husband. He will not forsake you. The Bible says, **"If ye be willing and obedient, ye shall eat the good of the land"** (Isa. 1:19). God is saying, "My Name is Jehovah Jireh. I am your provider. That job cannot support you like I want you supported. Turn to Me."

You don't need support from this world system. Get on God's Word. His Word is your support. If you feed on His Word, reading and meditating on it, it will become Spirit and life to you (John 6:63). It will cause things to happen in your life when there was no other way for them to happen.

God is your Father. He gave you His Word. He is your provider, and He wants you to look to Him and bring everything to Him in prayer. Stop going to others for help. Talk to your Father about it. Tell Him what your needs are and then depend on Him to get the job done for you. Didn't He say, "I will never leave you or forsake you" (Heb. 13:5)? Didn't He say, "I am not a man that I should lie. If I said it, I'll make it good" (Num. 23:19)?

God wants you to rise up and partake of His fullness. You are qualified if you've been born into the Kingdom of God. Just use your God-given authority. Jesus is your Elder Brother. He's your Savior and Lord. You're an heir of God — a joint-heir with Jesus. God is your Heavenly Father. You can depend on Him and Him alone, and He will take care of you.

God is real, and every word He said, He meant. The world system has tried to break us down. Religion and the doctrines of men have had us settling for less and living below God's standards for us. But, I tell you, we are not spiritual stepchildren with nowhere to turn for help. How can we be when our Father has said, "The earth is Mine and the fullness thereof" (Ps. 50:12)?

Don't Lean on the Arm of Flesh

You see, the problem has been, we've depended on everyone else but Daddy. We've filled out every form and application but the one Daddy told us to "fill out." We've walked by sight and not by faith. We've walked in the flesh and not in the Spirit. We've trusted everyone else but Daddy when His Word has told us, **"Trust in the Lord with all thine heart; and lean not unto thine own understanding"** (Prov. 3:5).

Learn to take the Word of God and be bold in your authority in Christ. Walking in your spiritual authority, life can be different — *better* — for you!

People talk about having all kinds of ministries, but they never talk about having a money ministry. And, yet, there is such a thing as a money ministry. God is looking for people to have this kind of ministry — a ministry of giving. Even if they are not rich, if they are willing and obedient, He will use what little they have and turn it into much.

You see, once God finds out that you will are willing and obedient with what you have, yielding it to Him, He will make you a money "reservoir" for Him. In other words, He will stack prosperity up in you. When the abundance starts coming in that capacity, and you are using that money for His work — as a money ministry — then He will let you have some of it too! In fact, the more faithful you are, I believe He'll say to you, "Go ahead and get out of there what you want. You won't hurt the supply." It's sort of like an account that He will just let you withdraw from. But you have to keep making deposits into His work. You can't just use money for your own cause.

Some people may read this and think, *How could God give me a money ministry?* No matter how "small" you think you are financially, you can enter into what I call a money ministry. You remember I told you that if you can take authority over your *giving*, you can take authority over your *receiving*. If you can faithfully *give* to God, then you can boldly *receive* from Him too.

Get hold of that truth. It doesn't always go over big with folks the first time they hear it if they are not giving as they should — if they are not taking authority over their giving to God.

Money will not come to you supernaturally in abundance without your giving.

Learn To Dedicate Your Money to the Lord

Now what exactly do I mean when I say "money ministry"? I'm talking about making your money a ministry unto the Lord. In other words, you're not just going to let the Lord have ten percent (although we are commanded in Malachi 3:10 that ten percent, the tithe, does belong to Him) of your income. And you're not just going to let Him have twenty, thirty, or forty percent. No, you're going to let Him have it *all* and talk to Him about what to do with it.

Some people are not receiving what they should be from the Lord even though they tithe, because they don't tithe in faith — they count that ten percent down to the penny — and they give nothing or next to nothing beyond the tithe. They are not pouring out of their resources to Him; therefore, they are not receiving an abundance of resources. Remember the Bible says, "...**He** which soweth sparingly shall reap also sparingly; and he which soweth bountifully shall reap also bountifully" (2 Cor. 9:6).

Do you know why the Lord wants you to give or dedicate and consecrate your money to Him? It gives Him a chance to pour out His blessings on you as He wants to pour them out on you. Dedicate your job to the Lord. Hold up your paycheck to Him and talk to Him about what to do with it. Then do what He tells you. (Some people can't do that today, because they owe all those department stores and credit-card companies. They need to tithe and pay their bills. Then they don't have anything left.)

Just as a bank has certain criteria it has to meet to handle money, we have certain criteria that we have to meet to handle God's money. It's not easy to dedicate all your money to the Lord, especially if you're used to being broke! When you get a little bit, you're grabbing for it, and you don't want to give it to somebody else. Often, we practice grabbing and holding on to money, scraping by the best we can instead of practicing dedication to the Lord with our money.

Your Money Is Your Substance

Let's look at Luke's Gospel at an example of some women who had a money ministry unto the Lord.

> And it came to pass afterward, that he went
> throughout every city and village, preaching and
> shewing the glad tidings of the kingdom of God:
> and the twelve were with him,
> And certain women, which had been healed of evil
> spirits and infirmities, Mary called Magdalene, out
> of whom went seven devils,
> And Joanna the wife of Chuza Herod's steward,
> and Susanna, and many others, WHICH
> MINISTERED UNTO HIM OF THEIR
> SUBSTANCE.
>
> LUKE 8:1-3

First, I want you to notice that Jesus was not broke
when He ministered in His earth walk! We know He had
a treasurer, Judas Iscariot. Well, to have a treasurer, one
has to have a treasury. So we know Jesus was not broke.
Also, it says right here in Luke 8 that these people Jesus
had ministered to "ministered unto Him of their
substance." That means they gave Jesus money.

Don't you know that the women in this passage whom
Jesus ministered to and set free were glad to be delivered?
And when they were delivered, they turned around and
"ministered unto Him of their substance" (v. 3). They
wanted to financially support the work of God so that
others could be delivered too. They wanted someone else
to receive the blessings they'd received, and they knew it
took money to do that.

Notice something else in verse 3. It says, **"...Joanna...and Susanna, and MANY OTHERS...."** Many others did what? They ministered unto the Lord with their substance. What does "minister" mean here? It means they provided Him with money from their substance — from their own financial resources.

In a Money Ministry, Your Blessing Reaches Others

Have you ever been healed or supernaturally blessed in some way by the Lord? When God blesses you, don't you desire that others be blessed in the same way you've been blessed? That's the way it is with a "money ministry." God blesses you financially, and you want to make sure others are blessed financially, too, especially those who are doing something for the Lord — those with gifts and callings on their lives who need money to fulfill the vision God has given them.

For example, an individual could have the call of God on his life, but to be in the ministry, he needs money for buildings, office equipment, and for his various outreaches, such as newsletters, radio, and television. Helping to finance the work of God through various ministers and ministries is part of having a money ministry.

Many people say they want to have a money ministry, but when they get blessed financially, they become selfish like the publican and the Pharisee we read about in the Gospels. They want God to give money to them through people, but they don't want to give any money away to others. They become concerned only with themselves and their needs and wants. Remember the farmer in Luke 12:13 through 21? He was just relaxing and basking in all his prosperity, talking about where he was going to build his next barn so he could hoard all his goods. He wasn't concerned about anyone else. God will not continue to bless selfish people.

A Blessing 'Relay'

If you've been ministered to by a ministry, you should minister financially to that ministry. (Of course, we are to always put our local church first. Our tithes go to our local church.) People often attend meetings, get blessed, and just run off. They dance, get happy, get healed, get their families straight, and then they run off without even considering giving an offering toward that meeting.

Why do you want to minister to the ministry that ministered to you? Because you want others to receive what you received. By contributing to that ministry, the "relay" of your blessing is a continual process, because the next person who receives from that ministry will do the same thing — contribute to the work of that ministry — and so on and so forth.

"Well," someone asked, "can you pay to be healed?" No, but when you are healed, you can show appreciation to the Kingdom of God by saying, "Let's make a wider path wherein more people can be healed."

I've told the story before, but the church I pastor was a small Baptist church years ago before the Lord dealt with me about changing the name and the direction of the church. The building we met in held about 200 people. When we stepped out and began Word of Life Christian Center, we started running about 550 people. We minister to thousands in the church we're in today.

You see, we are ministering to more people now. Our ministry has a broader value, but it took money to get us to this place. People had to give money to enable us to do what we are doing today. Prayers alone wouldn't do it. The contractors who built our church didn't want prayers — they wanted to get paid!

Now as a minister, there's a time to receive money and a time *not* to receive money. If there has ever been a time when I thought a person was trying to pay for what the Lord had done, I've said, "Nope, I can't take your money."

You can't pay for what the Lord has done. Great men of God have died ahead of their time because they used the opportunity when God was moving and blessing and healing people to stop and take up offerings. That's the wrong time and the wrong way to receive money, and they eventually died as a result because they wouldn't judge and correct themselves.

Ministers shouldn't go after money. If they do, they are in error. Ministers must go after souls and after getting people set free. Certainly, you need plenty of money to have a large ministry, but God will supply it. There is a right time to receive offerings, and people should support the work of God that is blessing and feeding them spiritually.

Your Money Ministry Shows Your Gratitude to the Lord

In Luke chapter 8 in the case of Mary Magdalene, from whom Jesus cast out seven devils, she was appreciative. I mean, one devil was enough, but this woman had seven! Have you ever been vexed by the devil? I mean, Mary Magdalene was glad to get rid of those devils and to be free, and she showed her gratitude to Jesus by ministering to Him with her substance. She became a devoted follower of God because of what He had done for her.

Now let's look in more detail at that word "substance." Substance usually means *something tangible*. In other words, those women in Luke chapter 8 ministered to Jesus with things that they had — material things. And I'm sure that included money.

You remember the girl in the Gospels who poured expensive perfume out on Jesus' feet and then wiped His feet with her hair? She ministered to Jesus with her substance. Then some turkey (Judas Iscariot) complained that she was wasting that perfume by pouring it out on Jesus' feet. But she was not wasting; she was showing her appreciation to the Lord.

You know, some people today will scrutinize ministers and talk about their lifestyles and accuse them of wasting money, especially if they think it's ministry money. For example, they will say, "Well, he shouldn't fly first-class; he should fly in the back of the plane. He's wasting money."

But what they don't understand is, most of the time when a minister flies first-class, he is protecting the anointing. When a minister comes to a meeting fresh, Heaven comes down on the people. But when he is bedraggled, tired, and worn out, it is more difficult for the anointing to flow properly. Besides, often, when a minister flies first-class, someone is paying for him to do so, because he appreciates his or her ministry and wants to do something nice. So people shouldn't judge a minister so quickly.

I think if anyone should fly first-class, it should be the preacher! I tell you, I am a big man, and I don't need to sit in a small seat in an airplane with my knees hitting my chin and two other people practically sitting on top of me! I can't even think straight, much less pray, in that kind of condition!

Many people just don't understand that. But you should want the man or woman of God to be comfortable. When they come to hold a meeting for you, you don't want them to have anything on their mind but Jesus. They shouldn't be concerned about money. Those women in Luke chapter 8 knew that. Their attitude was, "The Lord shouldn't be concerned about money. Anyone who can bring this type of deliverance, we want other people to get in on it, so let's become partners with Him. He has to have money to travel to all these different places with His disciples. Let's minister unto Him with our substance."

I'm talking about having a money ministry and about taking authority over your giving so you can take authority over your receiving. Some people have never reached this place of decision and commitment because they have been "smothered" in the past by preachers with wrong motives trying to coerce them to give. Those ministers weren't trusting in the Lord; they were trusting in the people.

But even though this happens, you as a giver — as a "money-minister" — need to get beyond seeing your giving as doing someone else a favor. You have to begin to see it as giving unto the Lord, and you have to see it as a privilege.

You Can't Out-Give God

I believe those ladies who became partners with Jesus in Luke chapter 8 had a money ministry. Their giving to Him of their substance put them in the category of having a money ministry and of receiving even more substance.

The Lord will never let you out-do or out-give Him. Do you know why? The Lord can't be in debt to any man. If you give in faith and obedience, He is always going to give more back to you, because you were obedient to Him and because you trusted Him. He wants you to depend on Him, and you can depend on Him. He will never let you down.

The reason many people don't have money is, they haven't been able to take authority over their giving. They haven't been able to fully trust the Lord to get it back to them when He asked them to give.

The more money these people make, the more they take. When they increase, they forget about the Lord. They forget that He is the giver of every good and perfect gift (James 1:17) and that He is the One who gives the power to get wealth (Deut. 8:18). They get over into what I call "paying the world and tipping the Lord." The Bible asks the question, "Will a man rob God?" (Mal. 3:8). People do rob God when they withhold tithes and offerings from the church and from the work of God.

God Is the Blessing Multiplier

God is able to turn your hundreds of dollars into thousands and your thousands into millions. Do you believe that? But you have to *let* Him do it. Prosperity is more than wearing fancy clothes and driving fancy cars. It's being in union or in business with God with your finances. It's giving when He says, "Give," and it's receiving from Him and His Word by faith because you know His will for you concerning money and you know that you've obeyed Him. You expect the blessings of God on your life. Many people wear fancy clothes and drive fancy cars, but they are not really prosperous. They don't have a money ministry; they are "tipping" the Lord.

Having a Money Ministry Begins
With a Firm Persuasion and a Quality Decision

God doesn't need your money, but He wants you to have a money ministry unto Him, supporting His work, so He can get more money back to you. But you can't just have a money ministry overnight. You start out in faith and you *develop* in having a money ministry. It starts with a firm persuasion and a quality decision. You don't just "try" having a money ministry, and then when the going gets rough, turn and run from your commitment. You have to have a strong belief in what God has said and what He will do. Remember Numbers 23:19 says, **"God is** not a man, that he should lie; neither the son of man, that he should repent: hath he said, and shall he not do it? or hath he spoken, and shall he not make it good?"

Another way you could say it is, you have to see it before you can have it. When I use the word "see," I'm not talking about seeing with your physical eyes. I'm talking about seeing with the eye of faith or with your spirit man, the man on the inside.

In Second Kings chapter 2, the prophet Elijah said to Elisha, "If you see me when I go, you can have my mantle or anointing." The Lord is saying to us, "If you can see it, you can have it."

'Lord, Make Me a Blessing'

That phrase, "Lord, make me a blessing," is a powerful one! Having that attitude will put you in the channel of flowing with God in such a way that God will take out all the stops in blessing you! But you have to say it and mean it from your heart. You can't just "try out" having that attitude; it can't just be lip service to God.

Notice what you're *not* saying when you say, "Lord, make me a blessing." You're *not* saying, "Lord, bless me." You see, the rich young ruler in Mark chapter 10 messed up because he wanted to be blessed, but he didn't want to be a blessing. The key to having a money ministry and having the finances necessary to live a blessed life yourself is found in this phrase, "Lord, make me a blessing."

Have you ever noticed that some spiritual things work in conjunction with natural things, such as seed-time and harvest — the planting or sowing of seed and the reaping of a harvest? But then, on the other hand, some spiritual things work just the opposite of the natural way or the world's way.

For example, the world's system is set up to get your hands on every dime you can and hoard it for yourself. The world can't comprehend giving something away to get something. No, they have to *take* something and then hold on to it to have something. A person who lives by this principle can't understand the attitude, *Lord, make me a blessing*, as a means of increasing. No, he would have to say, "Lord, *give* me something. That's the only way I'm going to increase."

God's spiritual laws often work opposite the laws of this land or the laws of the world's system. The world will lie, cheat, steal, withhold, and do everything they can to get ahead. But God tells us to give it up! He tells us to, **"Give, and it shall be given unto you; good measure, pressed down, and shaken together, and running over, shall men give into your bosom. For with the same measure that ye mete withal it shall be measured to you again"** (Luke 6:38).

When the Lord knows that you sincerely desire to be a blessing, He won't have anything against your being blessed. In fact, you can't be a blessing to others without being blessed yourself. With the attitude, *Lord, make me a blessing,* your blessing can't become a curse to you. Money will never have or own you when you have that attitude. That attitude will keep you from error concerning money.

Money Extremes

There are extremes on both sides concerning the issue of money and divine prosperity. Some Christians are too focused on money; others think having money is a sin. I remember when I first began pastoring. We didn't take up offerings the traditional way by passing an offering plate or bucket. We had locked boxes hung on the walls of the church sanctuary, and the people could slip money into the slots. Then the deacons would take the boxes off the wall and count the offerings.

You see, I was so messed up in my thinking about money that I didn't want to be bothered with offerings. I didn't see the connection between money and the ministry, and I certainly didn't have the revelation of giving and receiving — of the people giving offerings and receiving blessings as a result.

I didn't want folks to think I was preaching for money, so I never said a word about money or offerings or about anything the church needed with which to bless and minister to people. So I would just preach and go back to my office and let the deacons take care of the money.

God saw my heart, but I was in error and in the ditch on one side of the road, so to speak. Money needs to be dealt with by preachers. It is a part of ministry. Money — tithing and the giving of offerings — is a part of God's people prospering and increasing supernaturally as He wants them to. In fact, God can't minister to you financially as He really wants to unless you are willing to minister to someone else. Many people don't qualify because they are tipping the Lord, giving that five- or ten-dollar bill every so often. Friend, that is not supporting the church or the work of God.

Your Money Ministry Extends To Fellow Believers Too

And when it comes to giving to fellow believers in obedience to the Lord, we need to qualify in that vein too. We need to take authority over our giving in that area as well as in the area of giving to the church and to ministers. For example, some Christians will hear God say to them, "Give that single mom a hundred dollars," and the first thing they want to do is judge her. They want to scrutinize her life to see if she is "worthy" of their hundred!

But that's not how the Lord works. If God told them to give it, she is worthy. They don't need to check up on her to see how many boyfriends she has or how many babies

she has. It doesn't matter how many babies she has —
one of those babies might need that hundred dollars!

I'm still talking about having a money ministry. When
you have a real money ministry unto the Lord, He calls
the shots. You don't just decide for yourself who you are
and are not going to give to. But when you practice
having a money ministry whereby God is running your
financial affairs, you won't have to go to the finance
company come Christmastime to borrow five hundred
dollars that could end up costing up to twice as much by
the time you pay it back!

When you sincerely, from your heart, ask God, "Make
me a blessing," He will do it!

> **Now the Lord had said unto Abram, Get thee out
> of thy country, and from thy kindred, and from thy
> father's house, unto a land that I will shew thee:
> And I will make of thee a great nation, and I will
> bless thee, and make thy name great; and THOU
> SHALT BE A BLESSING.**
>
> **GENESIS 12:1,2**

I believe that God blesses people so that they can be a
blessing, and that's the way you keep the blessings
flowing. A person could have money but not be a blessing
to others with it and miss out on the real blessings of
God. His family could break up. Other things could go
wrong with seemingly no way to straighten them out.

Money in itself is not evil, but it can bring evil if you act evil with it and refuse to give to God.

Do you want to be a blessing? It's hard to be a blessing until you're blessed with money. God wants to bless the Body of Christ and put money into their hands, but He has to get those hands to close *and* open. In other words, when they receive money, they can't just clench their fists on that money! They have to learn how to open that hand up when the Lord tells them to.

When You Increase, Keep a Humble Attitude And Remember That It Was God Who Blessed You

Some broke people get a little bit of money and start looking down on poor folks. They have the attitude, *I wonder what the poor folks are going to do. I made it.* Some successful businessmen will come into the church and rear their head back in pride because they gave five hundred dollars. Really, they should have given five *thousand*. God didn't tell us just to "Be blessed." He said, "And thou shalt be a blessing."

God has plans for you to have money. Remember I quoted Jeremiah 29:11, which says, **"For I know the thoughts that I think toward you, saith the Lord, thoughts of peace, and not of evil, to give you an expected end."** But His plan can't come through unless you cooperate with it.

You might say, "Well, I don't have much." Start where you are. God can take a little and make much out of it. I'm a living witness. When I met and married my wife, I was broke. She didn't know it because I was driving a big shiny car and flashed a few twenties in my wallet and sent her sandwiches every night where she worked. She thought I had it all, but I didn't have a quarter. I was so broke that I would have left me had I found out I was that broke! I was too broke to pay attention. Now *that's* broke!

A Money Grace

We've heard about the grace of God in connection with just about every area of our lives except money. But I believe God can grace us to increase in money — in financial prosperity.

> **Therefore, as ye abound in every thing, in faith, and utterance, and knowledge, and in all diligence, and in your love to us, see that ye abound** [increase greatly] **in this grace also.**
> **2 CORINTHIANS 8:7**

Paul was exhorting the Church at Corinth, but it applies to the Church of the Lord Jesus Christ today. First, he said, "Just as you have abounded in other things, such as faith...."

Well, we have come a long way in faith, haven't we? We know that the just shall live by faith and that without faith it is impossible to please God (Heb. 11:6). We know that that which is not of faith is sin (Rom. 14:23). We know that faith comes by hearing and hearing by the Word of God (Rom. 10:17). We know how to walk by faith. We know that you release your faith with your heart and your mouth connected (Mark 11:23,24). We know a lot about faith. We know that by faith we can be saved, healed, and delivered.

We also have some knowledge about salvation. We know about the blood of Jesus and that we can claim or plead the Blood. We know that we overcome the enemy, the devil, by the blood of the Lamb and the word of our testimony (Rev. 12:11). So we have some knowledge. Yet we are still broke.

Going back to Second Corinthians 8:7, Paul said, "See that you abound in this grace also." What grace was Paul talking about? He was obviously talking about a particular kind of grace that we needed to increase in. He was saying, "Along with increasing your faith, utterance, knowledge, and diligence, increase in this area too."

Well, what other area are we supposed to increase in? Verse 9 gives the answer.

For ye know the GRACE of our Lord Jesus Christ, that, though he was rich, yet for your sakes he

became poor, THAT YE THROUGH HIS POVERTY MIGHT BE RICH.

2 CORINTHIANS 8:9

You can't walk in the blessings of God fully without having some knowledge about those blessings. Your faith can't go beyond your actual knowledge of the Word. For example, most believers know the scriptures that talk about their salvation. They have the revelation in their spirit, and you couldn't talk them out of their salvation if you tried.

And many believers have a thorough knowledge of healing from the Scriptures. They know that they know that they know that with Jesus' stripes they were healed (Isa. 53:5; Matt. 8:17; 1 Peter 2:24). You couldn't talk them out of their healing if you tried.

But why are so many in the Church broke? Because they don't have the proper knowledge of the Word concerning divine prosperity, and the devil and religious traditions of men are talking them out of this blessing that God provided for them in redemption.

God wants us to abound or increase greatly in prosperity as well as all those other things Second Corinthians 8:7 talks about. It starts with knowledge of the Word concerning prosperity. Then you have to act on that knowledge. You have to actually tithe and give and believe God for increase to come to you in this area. You have to take authority over your giving so you can take authority over your receiving.

To Qualify for a Money Ministry, You Have To Go Beyond the Tithe on to Offerings

Many people tithe religiously, but they're not really using their faith with their tithing. If they were, they would be seeing some results.

> **Bring ye all the tithes into the storehouse, that there may be meat in mine house, and prove me now herewith, saith the Lord of hosts, if I will not open you the windows of heaven, and pour you out a blessing, that there shall not be room enough to receive it.**
>
> **And I will rebuke the devourer for your sakes, and he shall not destroy the fruits of your ground; neither shall your vine cast her fruit before the time in the field, saith the Lord of hosts.**
>
> **MALACHI 3:10,11**

They tithe religiously but not in faith, and they don't see any fruition of their tithing. Then, many times, people become so accustomed to tithing, but they stubbornly refuse to go any further with God. God's Spirit is dealing with them about doing something extra — about giving offerings — but they dig their feet in the ground with the attitude, "No, I'm not going any further. I'm not giving a quarter beyond my tithe."

People like that who are "holding God to the penny" are dangerous and can't be trusted with money. If God prospered some people who are like that, they would go off and leave Him. It would almost be like He was paying them to leave Him, and He won't do that.

A *Giving* Grace Produces a *Money* Grace

How do you "abound in this grace also" — in the money grace? By your giving. By your having a money ministry unto the Lord.

> **Moreover, brethren, we do you to wit of the GRACE of God bestowed on the churches of Macedonia;**
> **How that in a great trial of affliction the abundance of their joy and their deep poverty abounded unto the riches of their LIBERALITY** [or generosity].
> **For to their power, I bear record, yea, and beyond their power they were willing of themselves;**
> **Praying us with much intreaty that we would receive THE GIFT, and take upon us the fellowship of the ministering to the saints.**
> **And this they did, not as we hoped, but first GAVE their own selves to the Lord, and unto us by the will of God.**

Insomuch that we desired Titus, that as he had begun, so he would also finish in you the same GRACE also.

2 CORINTHIANS 8:1-6

Look at verse 1: *"...we do you to wit of the GRACE of God bestowed on the churches...."* Do you know what kind of grace Paul is talking about? He was talking about a *giving* grace. In other words, the Lord is doing you a favor letting you use your money on His behalf. You see, that money is His money that He has permitted you to have. And He wants to use you as a channel or pipeline to get finances to His work so He can get more finances back to you.

Every time you use your money on God's behalf, it gives Him the opportunity to give you more money!

Now look at verse 2 of Second Corinthians 8: **"How that in a great trial of affliction the abundance of their joy and their deep poverty abounded** [increased greatly] **unto the riches of their liberality."** Their liberality brought them out of poverty. They were liberal in their giving even though they didn't have a whole lot to give.

Paul was talking about money in this passage. He was talking about a giving grace.

Look at one more passage in Second Corinthians.

[Remember] this: he who sows sparingly and
grudgingly will also reap sparingly and
grudgingly, and he who sows generously [that
blessings may come to someone] will also reap
generously and with blessings.
Let each one [give] as he has made up his own
mind and purposed in his heart, not reluctantly or
sorrowfully or under compulsion, for God loves
(He takes pleasure in, prizes above other things,
and is unwilling to abandon or to do without) a
cheerful (joyous, "prompt to do it") giver [whose
heart is in his giving.]

                    2 CORINTHIANS 9:6,7 (*Amplified*)

You see, you have to get over into that giving grace
before you can get into the receiving grace. There are no
shortcuts. You can't receive first and *then* give. It doesn't
work that way.

The Lord recently showed me something interesting
about sowing and reaping. I was just walking through my
house one day, and it "hit" me. I said to my wife, "Did
you know that the earth doesn't need any seed? We put
seed into the earth because we need the earth to kick
something up for us out of that seed. But the earth
doesn't need any seed for itself. The earth will go on
being the earth with or without any seed."

As we already read in *The Amplified Bible*, Second
Corinthians 9:6 shows the results of sowing and reaping.

> But this I say, He which soweth sparingly shall
> reap also sparingly; and he which soweth
> bountifully shall reap also bountifully.
>
> **2 CORINTHIANS 9:6**

In order to operate in that giving grace, you have to do what the Lord tells you to do with money, and you have to be willing and "prompt to do it." For example, I was in a meeting once, and the Lord spoke to me to take someone's nineteen-year-old daughter shopping and let her "shop till she dropped"! My wife and I and my daughter took her. We were determined to obey God willingly and to have a money ministry unto Him.

This teen-aged girl shopped for about two or three hours, and when she was finished, I told my wife, "Write the check." I was happy to do it. It didn't make any difference to me how much it cost; I was under instruction from the Lord. I was under "arrest," so to speak, by the Lord, because anyone who knows me knows I don't like to shop! I like to go in, get what I want, and be out of there in twenty minutes. If I go into a store and don't see what I want, I turn around and head back to my car. But I sat there that day for about two or three hours, and I was content.

'How Much More?'

Let me tell you something else about that situation. I was blessed to be able to do that for that young girl just as I am glad to bless my own daughter and let her "shop till she drops." Well, what do you think about our Heavenly Father? Matthew 7:11 says, **"If ye then, being evil** [or natural]**, know how to give good gifts unto your children, HOW MUCH MORE shall your Father which is in heaven give good things to them that ask him?"**

How much more. How much more does your Heavenly Father want to bless you? It is the Father's desire that His children show Him strong in the earth's realm. Deuteronomy 28:10 implies, "All the people of the earth shall see that you are blessed." And Psalm 35:27 says, **"Let them shout for joy, and be glad, that favour my righteous cause: yea, let them say continually, Let the Lord be magnified, which hath pleasure in the prosperity of his servant."**

Is your Heavenly Father able to prosper you? Is He willing? In other words, will He do it for you?

Let me ask you another question. If you are a parent, do you like to see your own children blessed? Well, how much more does your Heavenly Father like to see you blessed? When the devil comes along and tells you what you can't have, you look him in the eye, so to speak, and say, *"How much more!* My Heavenly Father wants me blessed, and He wants to make me a blessing!"

Your Faith Can Bring You From Test to Triumph in Your Finances!

7

What does the Lord really want for the Church in the area of money? Often when we talk about money in the Church, believers get worried instead of spiritual! I mean, they get quiet when they should get excited! Why? Because, as I said, many Christians associate money with the world and not with God. They think money is worldly, yet they use it every day to function in life. (And some even use more than they have and obtain a facade or a false front of prosperity. Actually, they are broke on credit! They strive, struggle, and strain to have houses, cars, and clothes — and purses with nothing in them! But when the man or woman of God tries to teach them about a *godly* prosperity, they get real quiet.)

God Is a 'Money Specialist'!

Actually, God is a "money specialist." He knows things about money that we will never know. No banker, analyst, or broker will ever know what the Lord knows about money. We've been messing around, depending on men only. But when we hook up with God and turn our money over to Him, we can go from test to triumph in our finances. I believe we can even get to the place where we can bypass the bank!

Banks want to loan you money so they can receive the interest on your repayment. They don't like it when you pay your loan off early, because they want that interest to accumulate. That's one of the ways they make money. I have actually seen bankers get mad because we paid off a church loan early. They were cold toward us because they weren't going to make the money off our loan that they thought they were.

When we built the church building we're in now, I had a banker pay me a visit, trying to loan us money. He said, "We're available to help."

I answered, "I certainly appreciate it, but I don't need any help."

He asked, "Well, how much is that new church going to cost you?"

"Over a million dollars," I said.

"How are you going to build it?" the man asked, amazed.

I said, "We're just going to pay for it." And our building was built with cash. Everything is paid for, and we are a long way from broke. That's a testimony to Jesus Christ.

God doesn't mind your having money. In fact, He doesn't mind your having *plenty* of money. We talked about the fact that He delights in the prosperity of His people (Ps. 35:27). But He doesn't want believers to get money and then forget about Him. He doesn't want them to become satisfied when they become better off than they were before, and then all they want to do is tithe and not be bothered with any more Kingdom business.

What does God want, then? He wants you to have money, but as I said in the last chapter, He wants your money to be a ministry unto Him.

Look at Acts chapter 13.

> Now there were in the church that was at Antioch certain prophets and teachers; as Barnabas, and Simeon that was called Niger, and Lucius of Cyrene, and Manaen, which had been brought up with Herod the tetrarch, and Saul.
> As they ministered to the Lord, and fasted, the Holy Ghost said, Separate me Barnabas and Saul for the work whereunto I have called them.
> And when they had fasted and prayed, and laid their hands on them, they sent them away.
>
> **ACTS 13:1-3**

Notice in verse 2 it says they ministered unto the Lord. That's actually talking about praise and worship. These men of God were praising God and calling on His Name. But I want to show you how you can minister to the Lord with your money.

God Is a Big-Time Giver!

Whatever you do for the Lord, He is going to flood you with blessings in that area, because you can never out-give God. God is the biggest giver there is. The Bible says, **"For God so loved the world, that he GAVE his only begotten Son, that whosoever believeth in him should not perish, but have everlasting life"** (John 3:16).

The Bible also says, **"He that spared not his own Son, but delivered him up for us all, how shall he not with him also freely give us all things?"** (Rom. 8:32). So we don't ever have to be concerned about whether or not God will give to us. God is a giver; He's a *big-time* giver!

Then why are we so often tight toward Him? Is it because we are afraid that if we give money, He can't or won't get money back to us? We can trust the Lord with our finances if we can trust Him with our spirits — if we can trust Him to save us, rescuing us from hell and the kingdom of darkness and translating us into the Kingdom of light. And we can trust Him with our finances if we can trust Him with our bodies — if we can trust Him for healing, health, protection, and preservation.

I tell you, I am a living witness to the fact that we can trust God with our money, and that He will bring us from test to triumph! But we have to have a certain attitude first. We have to have the attitude that not only does ten percent of our increase belong to Him (Mal. 3:10), but the other ninety percent is His too! We need to turn it all over to Him so He can direct us to use it as He sees fit.

It's Faith *and* Action That Bring Results

We've been talking about having a money ministry and getting money loosed unto you as you loose what you have unto God and His work. As I said, you have to qualify to have divine prosperity. You have to qualify with your giving, but you have to qualify with your mouth too. In other words, you have to believe right, according to the Word, and you have to talk right. You can't just give and then say, "I need more money. How in the world is God going to get it to me?" No, the Bible says that God shall supply your need according to His riches in glory (Phil. 4:19), and the Lord is your Shepherd; you shall not want (Ps. 23:1). You have to believe and talk in line with the Word to qualify for divine prosperity.

On the other hand, you could confess the Word all you want, but if Jesus is not Lord of your finances — if He can't get you to turn loose of your tithes and offerings — prosperity is not going to come your way. We have to qualify both ways: with our faith and with our actions.

There's no reason for a good child of God — one who is obeying God — to be broke. It just isn't right when God's children are broke and in poverty and lack. You remember, the Bible says, **"If ye then, being evil, know how to give good gifts unto your children, how much** more shall your Father which is in heaven give good things to them that ask him?" (Matt. 7:11). Yet many of God's children call their "Daddy" a liar, because they don't have any confidence in His willingness and ability to bless them, and they're always "poor-mouthing," talking about what they don't have.

We let the world laugh at our "Daddy" — at our Heavenly Father. The world has seen God's people poor and downtrodden, and they've said, "I don't want to become a Christian. I figure I'm doing better than they are. What do I want with their God?"

But there's a brand-new breed of believer rising up who is not going to let religion, men's theology, and wrong teaching hold them back anymore. They have made up their minds that they want the real thing. They want all the things of God, and they are determined to go all the way with Him and to stop giving Him a bad name, so to speak, by their lack of faith.

God is bigger than our situations and circumstances. He is bigger than the poverty that has tried to rule and reign over us. The Bible says, **"For if by one man's offence death reigned by one; much more they which receive abundance of grace and of the gift of righteousness shall REIGN IN LIFE by one, Jesus Christ"** (Rom. 5:17).

So we know that God is bigger, and we know that *we* are to reign in life over circumstances instead of circumstances reigning over *us*. And we know that God's ways and His thoughts are higher, because Isaiah 55:8 and 9 says, **"For my thoughts are not your thoughts, neither are your ways my ways, saith the Lord. For as the heavens are higher than the earth, so are my ways higher than your ways, and my thoughts than your thoughts."**

I'm so glad about that, aren't you? I'm so glad I don't have to mess with religious teaching that would tell me that I have to be broke, sick, lost, and undone in life.

You Need a *Surplus* To Be a *Supplier!*

Why does God want to turn our money into a ministry unto Him? Some people with a little money in the bank are satisfied because their basic needs are met. They think, *That preacher isn't talking to me. I don't need prosperity; I have enough to get by.* But God wants us to have more than just enough. He wants us to have a *surplus* so we can be a *supplier*!

Do you remember what happened to Peter when he turned his money — his fishing boat whereby he earned his livelihood — into a ministry unto the Lord? Although Peter and his men had fished all night and had caught nothing, when Jesus told him to launch out again, they caught so many fish that the boats started to sink (Luke 5:7)!

Well, just as the Lord knows where the fish are, He knows where the money is. I want to look at something else that happened to Peter when he turned his money into a ministry unto the Lord. Look at Matthew chapter 17.

> And when they were come to Capernaum, they that received tribute money came to Peter, and said, Doth not your master pay tribute?
> He saith, Yes. And when he was come into the house, Jesus prevented him, saying, What thinkest thou, Simon? of whom do the kings of the earth take custom or tribute? of their own children, or of strangers?
> Peter saith unto him, Of strangers. Jesus saith unto him, Then are the children free.
> Notwithstanding, lest we should offend them, go thou to the sea, and cast an hook, and take up the fish that first cometh up; and when thou hast opened his mouth, thou shalt find a piece of money: that take, and give unto them for me and thee.
>
> **MATTHEW 17:24-27**

Let's look at the last verse of that passage, verse 27: "Notwithstanding, lest we should offend them, go thou to the sea, and cast an hook, and take up THE FISH THAT FIRST COMETH UP; and when thou hast opened his mouth, thou shalt find a piece of money: that take, and give unto them for me and thee."

I want you to notice something about what the Lord used to get money to Peter — a fish! I mean, that was a "called" fish. It was called by the Lord, summoned by the supernatural power of God — to "come up first" with that money in its mouth!

In this verse, the Lord Jesus showed that He can control the system on behalf of those who trust Him!

Now Peter had been a fisherman for a long time, but I bet he never caught a fish with money in its mouth! No, what happened to him in verse 27 was a miracle, and it shows that God has control over things. What we have to realize today is, God has control, but he needs someone to give Him some faith to work with to be able to show Himself strong on his behalf.

If you will give God your faith, your obedience, your confession, and, most of all, your heart, there is no limit to what He will do for you.

Faith Is of the Heart, Not of the Mind

Years ago, as I was just getting started in the ministry I have today, the Lord told me to quit my secular job. I didn't have sufficient funds stored up to be able to quit a job, but I obeyed the Lord. My mind said, *You're crazy!* But I "suspended" my mind and just let my spirit, my inner man, take over. I let my spirit man dominate my thinking, and I got to the place where I couldn't go backward in time and regret leaving or even think about what I was going to do. I had heard from the Lord. I had His peace, and He showed up strong in our lives, providing for us every step of the way.

Now don't you quit your job just because I or someone else did it. Let God tell you what to do in life. But when He talks to you and gives you certain instructions, don't let your flesh or anything in the natural keep you from doing what God told you to do. Do what God says to do. Give what He says to give and to whom He says to give it. Your responsibility is to obey; His responsibility is to bring it back in to you.

In the last chapter, we talked about the fact that it's the grace of giving that activates the grace of receiving. Your giving in faith moves the hand of God in your finances. You might say, "Well, I have been giving." Then add some faith to your giving and keep your heart right toward God. Don't let sin and wrong attitudes and thoughts of the heart tie you up in your finances.

When your heart and your mouth are working right, there is no such thing as your not receiving. The devil is not big or strong enough to hold you up indefinitely when you are operating in faith and obedience from a good, honest, and willing heart.

Where Is Your Focus — On the Problem or on God's Word?

Someone said, "Reverend Thompson, something is tying me up." Well, one problem could be your focus. You may be believing God's Word and striving to keep a pure heart before Him. But you may have your mind on your bills. You may have your mind on your test — your trouble — instead of on the triumph that God wants to bring you into.

Did you know that worry is a sin? Some people can have their mind on their problem so much that they can't see God. Their problem keeps getting bigger and bigger because that's what they're focusing on.

If you have bills piling up, lay those bills down and stop worrying about them. Trust God that they're going to get paid and just seek Him. Let Him show you how to give your way out of debt. You have to do it in faith. But when you give in faith, God will meet you.

Someone said, "I want to learn to give my way out of debt, but I don't have anything to give." Start cutting back on unnecessary spending. Then use some of that money for giving. You don't have to run out and buy a new suit of clothes because everyone else is doing it. Wear what you have and get ahold of this revelation. Before long, you'll be able to buy a new wardrobe!

Some people want to wait until they have more money in order to give. But you have to start where you are today. If you're always hoarding money and holding on tight to it, you'll never prosper in the way God wants you to prosper. When you're grabbing at money, you don't get money. Money goes away from you! There's a spirit of resistance to money around a person who's grabbing for money as if he's needy.

For example, you might be in a restaurant, and someone may feel inspired to pick up your check. But as he's walking over to your table, you're crying out on the inside, *"Take my check. Please take my check!"* You're shouting so much on the inside, *"Take it, p-l-e-a-s-e"* that the person who was going to pick up your check changes his mind and heads back to his table.

I believe people can sense a beggarly attitude. When I was broke, no one ever picked up my check at a restaurant until I learned to walk by faith. When I got in faith concerning finances, I acted as calm and confident as I could be — as if I had all the money in the world. I wasn't looking for a handout. I didn't see myself as poor; I saw myself rich. Now I can hardly go to a restaurant without someone wanting to pick up my check.

I am convinced that if people really knew God, they wouldn't have a worry in the world about anything, including money. Sometimes it takes being in a tight spot and having the Lord deliver you to see how good, faithful, strong, and mighty God is.

God has taken me out of some of the tightest spots financially that a person could be in. I have faced financial burdens and crises on every side. But, each time, I stood on the Word and confessed, "God will bring me out of this thing."

I've been cheated financially, sued, mocked, and ridiculed. I can just imagine that every demon in hell was dancing around me at times, having a party. I would just keep praying in tongues and looking to God. I didn't tell man my situation or go to anyone else but the Lord for help. Some of my family members would come by, and I'd say, "Everything is fine." I said that, not because everything looked fine in the natural, because it didn't. I said that because that's what I believed. So I just kept saying it.

You see, you can't go to man if you expect God to do something for you. You'll never know the faithfulness of God — you'll never know that He will bring you out — unless you trust Him in a tight spot. It may look as if nothing is happening, but God will turn some things around for you. Right in the middle of the storm, you have to look to Him. You have to continue to use your faith. And you have to pass the test and keep an obedient heart concerning giving. Even when the going gets rough, God will never let you down. You might be hurting, but you can have the last laugh. God's Word is the last word. It's the final authority.

You might even weep at times at night, feeling all alone in your situation. But joy comes in the morning (Ps. 30:5). You are not alone, for greater is He who is in you than he that is in the world (1 John 4:4).

I tell you, God is real, and the Bible is true! So don't give up. Don't quit. Keep confessing the Word. Keep worshipping and praising God. Keep shouting the victory. There's not enough demons or enough creditors to keep you down and defeated. It may take you a while. But don't quit. Just keep doing a little something concerning giving. Don't back off your giving, and don't back off your faith. If you were believing God for a house, keep looking at houses. Look at bigger houses than the ones you've been looking at!

You can't be a quitter and have money loosed unto you. You have to consistently do what you know to do from God's Word to realize the benefit of God's provision for you. *But you can do it!* You can go from test to triumph in your finances. You can say and mean from your heart, "Money, thou art mine! Money cometh to me now! Money, thou art *loosed!*"

About the Author

Dr. Leroy Thompson Sr. is the pastor and founder of Word of Life Christian Center in Darrow, Louisiana, a growing and thriving body of believers from various walks of life. He has been in the ministry for twenty-two years, serving for twenty years as a pastor. Even though he completed his undergraduate degree and theology doctorate and was an instructor for several years at a Christian Bible college in Louisiana, it wasn't until 1983, when he received the baptism in the Holy Spirit, that the revelation knowledge of God's Word changed his life, and and it continues to increase his ministry. Dr. Thompson attributes the success of his life and ministry to his reliance on the Word of God and to being filled with the Holy Spirit and led by the Spirit of God. Today Dr. Thompson travels across the United States taking the message of ministerial excellence, dedication, and discipline to the Body of Christ.

Other Books by Dr. Leroy Thompson Sr.

Money Cometh to the Body of Christ!

The Voice of Jesus:
Speaking God's Word With Authority

What To Do When Your Faith Is Challenged

How To Find Your Wealthy Place

To order,
write or call:

Ever Increasing Word Ministries
P. O. Box 7
Darrow, LA 70725

1 (888) 238-WORD
(9673)

To contact Dr. Leroy Thompson Sr.,
write:

Dr. Leroy Thompson Sr.
Ever Increasing Word Ministries
P. O. Box 7
Darrow, Louisiana 70725

Please include your prayer requests
and comments when you write.

To obtain a free catalog of Dr. Thompson's teaching materials
or to receive a free quarterly newsletter, write to the address above.